ANTARCTICA
A DIFFERENT ADVENTURE

JASON KIMBERLEY

Hardie Grant Books

Patriot Hills

Every effort has been made to incorporate correct information and statistics, and to contact the owners of copyright for permission to reproduce material which falls under the 1968 Copyright Act. The author and publisher regret any errors and omissions and invite readers to contribute up to date and/or additional relevant information to Hardie Grant Books. Omissions will be rectified in subsequent editions.

Published in Australia in 2007 by
Hardie Grant Books
85 High Street
Prahran, Victoria 3181, Australia
www.hardiegrant.com.au

ISBN 978 174066 534 6 (hb)
ISBN 978 174066 525 4 (pb)

Cataloguing-in-Publication data is available from the National Library of Australia

Cover photography by Jason Kimberley
Cover, internal design and typesetting by Traffic Design Studios
Printed and bound in China by SNP Leefung on 140gsm NEP matt art paper
Papers used by Hardie Grant Books are natural, recyclable products
made from wood grown in plantation forests.

10 9 8 7 6 5 4 3 2 1

PRAISE FOR AUSTRALIA EXPOSED BY JASON KIMBERLEY

'There are not many words – they are not necessary. Each picture is a story in itself;
each a scene that will challenge the imagination and probably send it flying.'
THE SUNDAY TIMES

'Jason's book encapsulates many things I love about Australia, things I had forgotten and
things I never knew existed. Jason has a unique combination of a wonderful eye and
sense of humour mixed with his obvious love of the subject – a touch of magic.'
HUGH JACKMAN

'*Australia Exposed* is a striking photographic journal. This inspiring book captures Kimberley's view
of Australia's heartland – its physical and emotional soul, its stark landscape and sturdy people.'
GQ

'Jason's work truly encapsulates the rawness, beauty and light of Australia.'
ERIC BANA

'Jason Kimberley reveals the wide brown land in all its glory and complexity ... Kimberley
provides a fresh perspective of one of the most inhospitable places on earth.'
HARPER'S BAZAAR

'Jason Kimberley has the photographer's eye. The jaundiced, half-squinted to the sun,
bush or beach, culturally specific, Australian photographer's eye. The humour, the straight-
forwardness, the mystery, he captures the essence of Australia and Australians.'
RUSSELL CROWE

'Jason's two-year photographic odyssey captures its essence in the most raw and
natural form. He takes the reader on a magical journey through an Australia
that few have ever seen and even fewer will ever experience.'
GREG NORMAN

'In his stunning book, *Australia Exposed*, self-taught Jason Kimberley
captures the unique, often harsh beauty of life in Australia.'
MARIE CLAIRE

'The best images in this book are the semi-abstract, beautifully composed forms that
make a visual poetry of blown-out tyres and rusty iron ... handsomely produced ... Buy
it and see a slice of the country – and support a bold publishing initiative.'
THE SUNDAY AGE

'Kimberley has captured a new dimension in the harsh beauty of the Australian landscape.'
THE SUNDAY TELEGRAPH

'Jason Kimberley's book illustrates the secret treasures of Australia. Only a true explorer can capture such rare and unique images. This book sits proudly on my coffee table as a beautiful reminder of home.'

'The images of human adaptation to the vastness and forces of primitive nature provoke, stimulate and inspire with their uncompromising clarity and colour. What was to have been a personal record of a journey for Jason, has become a "cultural text" for everyone.'

'The result is a stunning book, *Australia Exposed*. But don't expect the obvious from Kimberley's look at life in Australia – there are no shots of the Opera House or Sydney Harbour Bridge, no sunsets and no Great Barrier Reef.'

'One of the strongest books exposing the beauty of the land is fittingly called *Australia Exposed* – a fantastic photo essay of our time.'

'*Australia Exposed* is more than a detached document of the alternately tough and lush Australian landscape. Kimberley's experience is embedded in the images.'

'You won't recognise many of the scenes in Jason Kimberley's photographs of Australia, but you will identify the colours and mood of the images as distinctly Australian.'

'A compelling set of photographs that speaks volumes.'

'This is one out of the box. I have covered so many books but I was taken to the locations in the book, transported through the images. This is the intention of any artist, photographic or otherwise.'

'You are quite a brave man, also bold and daring! It amazes me how you bring out the colours of the landscapes in your photographs.'

'One can't help but draw parallels to another famed photographer, Ansel Adams. Preferring a certain unrehearsed rawness in his subjects, the pictures have a certain reality while Adams' photographs seek to exalt nature; Kimberley strives to make her accessible with hints of human elements in each frame. His ability to capture succinctly the subtle details reveals an evolved appreciation.'

CONTENTS

Minaret Peak

FOREWORD

Jason Kimberley's book, *Antarctica: A Different Adventure*, is informative, beautiful and fun. It is a book that will make you smile and make you laugh. However, there is also poignancy – Antarctica and the great Antarctic web of life surrounding it are bearing witness to profound climate change.

Ice cores sunk deep into the Antarctic ice shelf reveal the 'breathing' of the planet, the rise and fall of carbon dioxide and life itself, cycling with remarkable regularity over the last several hundred thousand years. These ice cores also reveal the equally remarkable rise in carbon dioxide following on from the industrial revolution and our exponential use of fossil fuels exacerbated by continuous land clearing.

In the Southern Ocean, dramatic changes are taking place. The ice shelves are melting and breaking away, destabilising the glaciers behind and raising the sea levels; and the ocean is slowly but surely acidifying as the carbon dioxide dissolves in the surface layers of the water. In addition, the numbers of krill – the shrimp-like crustaceans upon which so much life in and around Antarctica depends – are dropping by the day.

We humans are actively warming the planet and are partly if not wholly responsible, yet we may still have time to avoid the worst effects. It will require us as nations to act selflessly and to act in concert.

In this last great wilderness, Jason Kimberley's soul was touched. The question now for us all is will we protect our natural home – or will we continue to let it degrade?

GREG BOURNE
CEO WORLD WILDLIFE FUND FOR NATURE AUSTRALIA

INTRODUCTION

I hate the cold. It invades your entire being – your mind, your body and your soul. In Antarctica, staying warm is an unremitting challenge, requiring your fullest attention every minute of the day. One of my greatest fears is that of being stuck, exposed and helpless and slowly freezing to death, in some lonely wasteland. I think this is one of the reasons that Antarctica has always intrigued me.

My attraction to heroic and often ill-fated adventure stories began in early childhood when I became absorbed by accounts of the much-maligned Burke and Wills expedition of 1860, which took the doomed explorers deep into the Australian interior. From here, my childhood fascination with death and tragedy led me to the famous race to the South Pole between the Englishman Robert Falcon Scott and his great rival, the Norwegian Roald Amundsen.

Thirty years after first hearing the tales of Scott and Amundsen's race to the pole, I found myself summoning all my courage and seriously contemplating making the trip to Antarctica. In August 2004, I sent a copy of my book *Australia Exposed* to my friend the respected and well-credentialed mountaineer and polar traveller Peter Hillary. I first met Peter in 1991 during preparations for our climb on Mount Aconcagua, the 6962-metre peak on the border of Chile and Argentina.

On receiving the book, Peter organised for us to catch up over lunch, where many things were discussed, including the possibility of a trip together to Antarctica. Peter mentioned that a climb of Mount Vinson, the highest peak on the continent, was in his plans and that he could be headed there within the next year. Wow! That certainly gave me something to think about.

My mind raced through the possibilities: who will come on the trip? How long will it take? How cold will it be? Will I be able to do it? Do I really want to do it? What will my wife, Caroline, think? After waiting a few days for the excitement to settle down, I started thinking what the trip would involve and what I wanted to get out of it.

My first call was to my old school mate Jason Veale. Jason and I have been close friends for many years and we have shared a love of adventure since we went spear-fishing and abalone-poaching together in our teens. We have since joined up to travel through the remote desert regions of Australia and to canoe down the upper Amazon in Peru. Jason was very keen on Antarctica, but not so thrilled about going up a mountain. Fair enough. I would see what I could do about that.

I formulated a new plan. 'Peter, what if we don't climb Mount Vinson but instead consider an old-fashioned Antarctic trek? My mate Jason Veale is excited by Antarctica but less than thrilled about climbing a mountain, and I have got to say that, in my mountaineering experience, the relief of getting to the top does not adequately compensate for the extreme unpleasantness of getting there. How do you feel about that?'

Peter was happy to take this away for further consideration. He called me back a week later, very excited about the new plans. He told me that he had made some enquiries and that it could be done. There is a logistics group, ALE, that flies into the Chilean sector of Antarctica and lands on a naturally occurring blue-ice runway. This is not a commercial flight but a Russian charter that operates for three months during the summer season from Punta Arenas at the southern tip of Chile. Right, we're in!

I need to take a step back here. In recent years, I have made some dramatic changes in my way of life. I had spent what seemed like a lifetime working in the clothing retail business, with diversions into home renovation and owning and operating the Veludo bar and restaurant in Melbourne before returning to the family business – Just Jeans. I had always felt a certain responsibility to do my bit for the family, but in doing this I felt somewhat unfulfilled in that I was not following my own dreams.

I have always wondered why children work in their parents' businesses. Is it just a remarkable coincidence? Do we love the same industry with the same passion as our fathers? Are we unwittingly pushed there? Does it just happen that way? Is there a certain feeling of obligation? The prospect of following in my father's footsteps always seemed unsatisfactory to me. Furthermore, as the son of the boss, you feel obliged to set a perfect example, work long hours, toe the company line, constantly travel around the country – in short, conform, which I am not very good at.

When the family decided to sell the business in 2002, I was at first a little disappointed that it was all over, but then the exhilarating feeling of total freedom washed over me. I thought about how this opportunity could be embraced in a way that would set me free to follow my own path. I had taken a series of photographs on a four-wheel-drive trip around Australia with Caroline in 2000. These photographs seemed to impress all who saw them, so I thought, am I onto something? I decided to self-publish a book, *Australia Exposed*, and exhibit the images. Within two years of its launch, the book had sold over 9000 copies, and the images had been exhibited successfully in Melbourne, Sydney, New York, Singapore, Seattle and Los Angeles. All of a sudden I had become 'Jason Kimberley, the photographer and author'. It has been without doubt one of the best decisions that I have made in my life.

With excitement and some trepidation, I wondered how to put my next adventure to Caroline. How would she react to me taking off for a month hauling a sledge across the frozen fields of Antarctica? Her first concern revolved around me being eaten by a polar bear. I assured her that this would not happen, as polar bears do not live in Antarctica. Her other concern was that I may fall down a crevasse and die. I could not offer too much comfort here other than a promise to be careful. She was also a 'little miffed' that we would not be able to share our first Antarctic experience together – she planned to take a scenic flight over the continent and view it from a safe distance. Eventually, all her concerns were allayed, and before long Caroline just felt proud and impressed that I would even take on such a challenge. Her final word on the subject was: 'It's not as if you are going to the Maldives to sit around a pool, get massages and sip fluffy drinks with umbrellas. If that were the case, I would insist on coming!'

Before going to Antarctica, I felt I should research what was happening there, and how developments on the frozen continent may affect our lives now and in the near future. I knew the hole in the ozone layer over Antarctica was growing at a rapid rate and that this was probably a cause for concern. I also knew that a large amount of the Earth's fresh water is stored there as ice – 70 per cent, as it turns out. Just think: all the rivers, all the lakes, all the dams and inland waterways, all the glaciers and all of the Arctic ice cap account for only 30 per cent of our freshwater. The rest is frozen on the Antarctic continent. Oh, and if all this ice were to melt somehow, sea levels would rise by 60–70 metres!

The more I read, the more concerned I became. The USA has recently cut a 1600-kilometre highway from their base at McMurdo on the Ross Sea coast to their base at the South Pole. In 2004, the Australian government put forward a claim for a massive undersea tract off the Australian Antarctic claim, with the ultimate aim of exploiting offshore resources. Not surprisingly, it was howled down by all the other signatories to the Antarctic Treaty. Australia was reminded that Antarctica is 'a nature reserve devoted to peace and science', not exploitation.

Tourists to Antarctica now number upwards of 30 000 per summer season, with the majority coming on cruise ships to the Antarctic Peninsular. These numbers are increasing at a rate of 13–17 per cent per annum. There are now 37 permanently manned stations on Antarctica and another thirteen that are occupied seasonally. The Japanese and Norwegians still slaughter whales here by the thousand for scientific purposes. Australia's Antarctic claim of 42 per cent of the continent is largely unrecognised by other nations, namely the USA, China and Russia, who have built bases on the Australian claim.

After a recent trip there, National Party Senator Barnaby Joyce made several observations: 'When you're away ... you realise that what is really important is the actual nature of people and the vastness of nature itself.' Well put, Senator; we do need to commit to preserving this pristine wilderness. He went on to say, 'What you have to ask is do I turn my head away and allow another country to exploit my resource, and do I just walk away from my territorial integrity of that claim, or do I position myself in such a way as they can't exploit it, or do I position myself in such a way as I'm going to exploit it myself before they get there?'

The senator's comments were derided by most of his colleagues, and by fellow senator Ross Lightfoot in particular, who said on ABC Radio, 'There's no chance of exploitation of ... any of the resources there, biological or mineral wise, and particularly oil ... I'm against it; the committee's against it; the Government is against it; the Labor Party is against it, and the United Nations is against it as well.' It is of great concern, nonetheless, that the 'do it before someone beats us to it' attitude exists at all. But in our short-sighted, self-interested, profit-driven world, isn't Antarctica just another resource to exploit?

Many years ago, back in 1982, I cut an article from a science magazine and have had it stuck on the wall above my desk ever since. It is one of those articles that compresses the life of our planet into a time frame that we can readily understand. It reads as follows:

If you were to condense this inconceivable time-span into an understandable concept we can liken the Earth to a person of 46 years of age. Nothing is known about the first four years of this person's life and, while only scattered information exists about the middle span, we do know that only at the age of 42 did the Earth begin to flower.

Dinosaurs and the great reptiles did not appear until one year ago, when the planet was 45. Mammals arrived only eight months ago; in the middle of last week man-like apes evolved into ape-like men, and at the weekend the last Ice Age enveloped the Earth. Modern Man has been around for four hours. During the last hour Man discovered agriculture. The industrial revolution began just a minute ago.

During those 60 seconds of biological time, Modern Man has made a rubbish pile out of Paradise. He has multiplied his numbers to plague proportions, caused the extinction of thousands of species of plants and animals, ransacked the planet for fuels and now stands like a brutish infant, gloating over his meteoric rise to ascendancy, on the brink of the final mass extinction and of effectively destroying this oasis of life in the solar system.

Is this a little dramatic? Perhaps for some, but the truth always hurts when it relates to us. In the past we could be excused for not understanding the implications of our actions, but now we have no excuse. It seems the only people disputing our situation are those with short-term vested interests in doing nothing, and in continuing to exploit resources and pollute the planet. Meanwhile, short-sighted governments avoid making hard decisions that may cause short-term job losses and votes. The sad thing is that there is no apparent plan. It may already be too late. Our day of reckoning may be closer than we think.

Dr Eric Wolff and his team from the British Antarctic Survey have been studying the East Antarctic ice core – the deepest ice core yet extracted. Inside the core are tiny air bubbles, dating back almost a million years, which are the weather and air records of our past. 'My point would be that there's nothing in the ice core that gives us any cause for comfort,' said Dr Wolff at the British Association's Science Festival. In simple terms, there is a direct correlation between climate change and the levels of carbon dioxide. The ice core shows that for the past 800 000 years, carbon dioxide levels have remained between 180 and 300 parts per million (ppm). Today they are at 380 ppm. 'In the past it had taken 1000 years for carbon dioxide levels to rise by 30 ppm during natural warming periods. It has risen by that much in the last seventeen years.'

What does this mean? According to Dr Wolff, 'There's nothing to suggest that the Earth will take care of the increase in carbon dioxide. The ice core suggests that the increase in carbon dioxide will definitely give us a climate change that will be dangerous.' He went on to say, 'We really are in a situation where something's happening that we don't have any analogue for in our records. It's an experiment we don't know the result of.' His measurements indicate that the extra carbon dioxide is coming from a fossil source (that is, the burning of fossil fuels) as a result of increased human activity. The ramifications of this are not completely understood, as noted by the British Antarctic Survey's Dr Corinne Le Quéré: 'For example, we don't know what the effect will be of ocean acidification on marine ecosystems. There is potential for deterioration.'

All the reading and research that I did before, during and after my 16 days of trekking, camping and man-hauling in Antarctica reminded me of an observation attributed to the Irish statesman Edmund Burke: 'It is necessary only for the good man to do nothing for evil to triumph.' Antarctica is a litmus test for us all. It holds the key to our climate history and is the last bastion of pristine wilderness on our planet. Our challenge is to preserve it. It is *our* environment, not just *the* environment.

Edwin Mickleburgh, who first visited Antarctica with the British Antarctic Survey in 1968, wrote in 1987 in his book *Beyond the Frozen Sea: Visions of Antarctica*, 'The continent has become a symbol of our time. The test of man's willingness to pull back from the destruction of the Antarctic wilderness is the test also of his willingness to avert destruction globally. If he cannot succeed in Antarctica he has little chance of success elsewhere.'

Antarctica is at once the most hostile and beautiful place I have ever been.

Chapter 1

PREPARATION BEGINS

The most daunting part of an Antarctic expedition is coming to terms with the training required to get fit enough for the physical challenges ahead. I despise the gym and have more of a 'let's sit in the shade and have a cold beer' attitude to training. So after several weeks of putting it off – rationalising the delay by telling myself, 'It's still five months away; I'll start next week' – I finally bite the bullet and book into a gym class with a personal trainer. To avoid running into anyone I know, I pick a gym several suburbs away. I choose a group session so I can hide in the corner when it becomes apparent that I am hopelessly out of condition.

The gym is new but has a low ceiling, poor ventilation and smells like my old school sports bag circa 1983. Just to get things going, the trainer, Chad, puts me on a machine that I am reliably informed is a cross-trainer; it has a running motion but without the impact. It also has upright handles that swing with the running action. I'm thinking, 'How easy is this?' Left right, left right – now I am building momentum, really getting the hang of it. How good?

'Hey Jason, what are you doing?' calls Chad. 'You're going backwards! You need to go forwards.' I am absolutely devastated at being exposed as the amateur I am. It doesn't bode well for my chances of travelling more than 200 kilometres across the snow and ice of Antarctica. Oh well, how much worse can it get?

After that setback, I find my feet and power ahead for ten minutes before being moved onto the bike. I feel a surge of pride as I manage to go forwards without assistance on my first try. My confidence is at an all-time high. Chad suggests a move to the weights. As I wrestle my weight-lifting demons, Chad asks me to lie down on a narrow bench. So far, so good. He then asks me to do five reps. I have no idea what this means, but I begin – or rather attempt – to lift the weights on the bar above my eyes. The bar shakes and wobbles around, as do my eyes, legs and arms. In fact the only part of me that doesn't shake is the middle of my back, which is pressed into the bench so firmly that movement is impossible.

Chad, seeing my distress, grabs the bar and eases it back into its cradle above my face. 'Bit heavy?' he asks politely.

'Impossibly heavy,' I gasp.

'OK, let me take some weight off for you.' The relief is enormous, without doubt the best thing that has happened to me all morning. I take a deep breath and prepare to try again.

As Chad adjusts the weights for my next attempt, I take several deep breaths. My psychological preparation has begun. Okay this time ... this time you can do it ... this time ... Arrgh! It's still too heavy. I can only manage one rep (which I have discovered stands for 'repetition') before Chad saves me from dropping the weight bar across my throat. 'Jason, I'll have to take some more weight off.' Chad kindly removes some more weights. On my third attempt, and with a greatly reduced weight, I focus on the bar and turn to Superman for inspiration: Up, up and away! The bar lifts up, once, twice, three times. I am unable to do any more.

The bar is pressing on my throat and slowly crushing my Adam's apple. My eyes dart around looking for Chad to help me remove the bar from my throat, but he is nowhere to be found. My head turns to the side, first the left and then the right, to assess the weights hanging at each end of the bar that is pinned to my throat. To my embarrassment there are no weights. I am lifting the bar only! A quick scan of the gym confirms that no one has witnessed my pathetic effort. There is nothing to do but laugh. Welcome to the wonderful world of weight-lifting.

After a few more visits to the gym, I am confident enough to move to a gym closer to home, my fear of discovery having evaporated. The new gym will be my second home for three days a week for the next four months.

Bogong Saddle

Rocky Valley Lake

After much discussion with Caroline about the type of trainer that I will need, we decide that a lean, ultra-fit fitness fanatic is the way to go. How wrong we are. My trainer for four months is to be Nick, who does not come close to fitting any of my original criteria for an ideal trainer. I quickly discover that laughter and entertainment are clearly the most important factors in getting through an hour-long session in the gym. We laugh our way through every hour, and the sessions pass in no time.

Before long, the laughter of the gym is replaced by the horror of the Victorian high country. Our first training weekend takes place at the Victorian ski resort of Falls Creek during the first weekend of September 2005. This is the first time that I have camped out and been trekking in the snow since my 1994 expedition to Mount McKinley, Alaska. It's a strange thing to be back in this unforgiving environment after such a long absence. I go thinking that I know it all, that I have all the skills, and consequently give my preparation very little time and almost no thought. My bags are packed hastily, but I have most of the things I'll need – after all, I have done this all before.

We arrive at the top car park at Falls Creek, aptly named Windy Corner, at dusk and begin to unload all our equipment. The amount of equipment required for such a trip always surprises me: equipment for cooking, for hiking, for skiing, for camping, for climbing, for photography, for carrying equipment ... Packing equipment for carrying equipment? It sounds so simple, yet oddly enough I have not considered this essential part of equipment. We load up our packs and sledges for the 'short haul to camp one'. Now, when I hear 'short haul', my mind starts to focus on, well, a short haul. I pack carelessly, with more than a hint of 'she'll be right, mate'.

There are three separate bags on my sledge, as well as some cooking equipment hooked onto the bags. The bags are unevenly weighted and loosely strapped on with some woefully inadequate thin cord. And then there are the skis and ski bindings that I have borrowed from Graeme Joy, who was the first Australian to reach the North Pole and kayak the east coast of Greenland, and who accompanied me on the Mount McKinley climb. Not that there is a problem with Graeme or his equipment. The problem is all mine. I have neglected to adjust his bindings for my boots. What an idiot! It is getting dark as the call is made to leave the car park and head off on our first trek as a team.

The first half hour passes without incident. We are on skis, hauling our sledges across ground that is either flat or slightly downward-sloping. How good is this? We reach the dam wall for the Rocky Valley Lake, which has a road running along the top of it. Sadly the snow has melted and we are forced to take off our skis and carry them. We also carry our sledges 300 metres to where the snow resumes again on the other side. It is my general belief that, when I am called upon to carry a load, one big weight carried once is vastly preferable to two lighter loads hauled twice. So off I trudge. This 300-metre haul is awkward at best. Lifting and carrying a fully loaded sledge is a very different experience from that of pulling it over slick snow and ice.

Falls Creek back country

Sastrugi

Mt Nelse – sun burning through fog

Eventually I make it to the end of the dam wall. By now sweat is pouring off me, and my poorly packed sledge has deteriorated to the extent that it needs a total repack and I need to have a serious think about how to move on from here.

It is now dark, −5°c and getting colder; my sledge is a disaster, and my trekking team mates are so far ahead that I can no longer see them. My entire body is steaming with sweat; my ski bindings and boots keep detaching, and I have no tool to tighten the bindings. Just to add insult to self-inflicted injury, it starts to snow, and my headlamp is – naturally – at the bottom of one of my three bags, but I have no idea which one. My frustration with my own lack of preparation is palpable. I unpack all the bags to find my headlamp and am somewhat surprised to find that the battery has not gone flat. It works. I don't!

After 20 minutes of mucking about and constant cursing, I get going again. While I have managed to repack everything, my sledge is still unstable and poorly organised, and my boots insist on slipping the bindings every time I put the slightest pressure on the ski edge. Over the next 500 metres, my skis pop off another three times. Furious at my gross incompetence, I decide that the skis will have to come off and be strapped to the sledge to avoid any further frustration. Ha!

The skis are tied down on the top of the sledge; the sledge is balanced as best as it can be, and off I go. After hauling the sledge another 200 metres, it starts to tip over again. I walk back to examine it, rebalance the top-heavy load with the problematic skis and continue to haul the accursed sledge over the dark, frozen track that winds its way along the shores of the Rocky Valley Lake. It is now more than two hours since we left the Windy Corner car park. After a dozen unwanted releases of the skis from the bindings followed by twenty sledge tip-overs, I am ready to explode with frustration or to curl up into a ball, surrendering to tears and inevitable death.

I have not seen Jason or Peter for more than an hour. Have they pulled off into the darkness without leaving a marker for me to follow? Have I been so preoccupied with my own woes that I missed the camp? Who knows? This is the peculiar thing about mountaineering and trekking. You work and move as a team but when things become a little difficult for whatever reason it becomes every man for himself. In my experience there is little waiting around and pandering to the slow and disorganised. You just catch up later. One thing that I do know is that the skis have to come off the sledge and will now have to be carried on my backpack as I cannot get them to balance with the tools available. I am on my hands and knees in the pitch black as snow falls around me; my headlamp is fading as I lash my skis to my backpack. My hands are beginning to freeze. I am not having fun yet.

I face a new challenge. Hauling the backpack, which now weighs over 50 kilos, onto my back with skis attached is most difficult, and requires me to bend down on one knee, sling it over one shoulder and then slide my opposite arm into the shoulder strap on the other side. My first three attempts see me fall on my face, driving the headlamp firmly into my forehead and causing some minor laceration. Now, rolling over, I am unsure whether to laugh or cry; I choose the former. Laughing at your own stupidity is helpful in that it focuses your attention on the fact that all of your problems are avoidable and that with proper planning and preparation this will never happen again.

Planning and preparation – this is a lesson that I believed I had learnt well on my first expedition in the Andes. So I am more than a little disappointed with myself that I have been forced to relearn it. I stagger into camp exhausted – four hours after leaving Windy Corner. The only good thing about being late into camp is that the others have already set it up and I can jump straight into the tent and a warm sleeping bag.

The next morning we pack up camp and I spend some time reorganising my clearly inadequate packing system for the day ahead. We have a relatively uneventful day, trekking up to the summit of Mount Nelse, an awesome peak thrusting 1884 metres into the crisp mountain air. To tell the truth, Mount Nelse is more of a hummock than a mountain, but as its name insists, it is nonetheless a mountain. On conquering Mount Nelse and adding it to my growing list of local summits – Mount Feathertop, Mount Dandenong, Mount Martha, Arthur's Seat (north face), Mount Buller and Mount Macedon – we rest for lunch. That afternoon, we undertake further training and run through all of our trekking gear, which is time well spent.

Crevasse rescue training

To observe Peter Hillary and Jason Veale living and working together is a source of joy and amusement. Peter Hillary is from mountaineering royalty. An accomplished climber, he has twice reached the summit of Everest, climbed on K2, climbed and guided expeditions on numerous peaks in the Himalayas, trekked to the South Pole and visited the North Pole with none other than Neil Armstrong, Steve Fossett and his father, Sir Edmund Hillary. He has also given countless lectures and motivational talks around the world on his adventures and what it is to live the life of an adventurer.

Peter is very reasoned and measured, a deep thinker from the 'measure twice, cut once' school of life. Jason Veale, on the other hand, is from the 'don't measure, just cut' school. Since meeting in 1981, Jason has been one of my dearest and closest friends, but his experience of mountaineering is mostly via the Discovery Channel. He also has a reputation for heavy-handedness when operating any kind of technical equipment. Jason's father, Warner Veale, has a large box full of electronic gadgets – watches, calculators, radios and so on – that Jason has broken, and Warner keeps this box as a reminder of the amusing and sometimes destructive youth his son enjoyed. 'Oh Jason, do you remember the time when you broke [insert item here]?' And so another story begins.

Day two on the mountain sees us doing some emergency-rescue training and general rope work. One of the first lessons is in how to attach an ascender to a rope (an ascender being a modern mountaineering tool for gripping onto a fixed rope with a handle to assist in hauling oneself up). We are also instructed how to attach a prusik to a rope in order to pull ourselves out of a crevasse (a prusik being the old and very difficult-to-use predecessor of the ascender, made by the climber out of rope, it is essentially a sling with a sliding friction knot).

As Jason has never done this before, most of the teaching is directed at him. I stand back, watch and wait. Peter has set up a rope slung over a high tree branch to simulate the situation in which one of us has fallen into a crevasse. All Jason needs to do is clip onto the rope and haul himself up into the tree. Unfortunately for Jason, Peter thinks it a good idea to try the dreaded prusik first, to provide a challenge. I struggle to hide my delight as I take up a prime position to witness the self-rescue attempt.

Jason looks very professional as he slips into his harness and hooks into the various ropes. As he leaves the ground, his harness tightens around his testicles, causing more than a little anguish. At Peter's suggestion, he rearranges himself before continuing. But now frustration takes hold as Jason is unable to operate a prusik. Jason can go neither up nor down, and Peter and I stand below giving advice. The prusiks are driving Jason mad. After several expletives, Peter finally lowers Jason from his suspended perch, exhausted after hanging by the rope for more than twenty minutes in his futile attempt to ascend.

Peter offers Jason the use of his ascender, which he gratefully accepts. This ascender has been with Peter for more than twenty years; it has been up Everest with him and is a prized piece of equipment. This time Jason climbs the rope with relative ease – up and down, up and down.

Ascender training

Mt Nelse summit approach

Summit of Mt Nelse in low cloud

On conquering the rope, Jason lowers himself down – almost to the ground. He accidentally locks up the ascender on the rope and is unable to move up or down. The pressure on Jason's testicles increases again and he becomes restless. Peter instructs Jason not to force the ascender's release button and says that he will lower him down. As the pressure on his testicles becomes greater and Jason's frustration grows to boiling point, I sense that something amusing is about to happen.

As Peter begins the process of lowering him, Jason reaches for a karabiner (a solid metal clip device with spring-loaded gate latch used for clipping on and off ropes, harnesses and so on). As he moves the karabiner towards the jammed ascender button, Peter reminds him again not to force the ascender under any circumstance. Ignoring Peter, Jason hooks the karabiner around the ascender button and pulls on it, gently at first, then with a little more vigour. Finally, at some point, moderate pulling gives way to forceful yanking, and as Jason applies maximum force to the button, it flies off at right angles, accompanied by a dramatic popping sound.

At this point I am falling about with laughter, unable to control myself. Some minutes later I look up to find one P. Hillary glaring at me accusingly. Quickly I attempt to give Peter a condensed rundown on Jason's heavy hand. Both Jason and I are fighting losing battles to keep straight faces, with Jason quietly whispering to me, 'Shut up. Will you just shut up? Oh my God, can you believe what I have done?'

Then something catches my eye in the snow. It is the small aluminium button, which has been sheared off at the base. 'Is this it?' I ask as the other two come in for closer inspection. 'It appears to have been sheared off with brute force,' I suggest. 'You bloody idiot,' Jason whispers angrily to me as Peter takes the button for further inspection. Shocked by Jason's rash destruction of his equipment, Peter can only offer, 'You just have to be so careful with the equipment. You cannot force these things.' This only adds to Jason's guilt and my giggling. Several minutes later, Peter repeats in bewilderment, 'It has just been sheared off …'

That night we sit in the tent as I cook dinner. When Peter enquires what we will be eating for our evening meal, I respond, 'katabatic hoosh!' This leaves Peter in stitches. Katabatic refers to the fierce polar wind that blows away from the South Pole, moving down the polar plateau that is produced by the cooling of the air at higher altitudes (the South Pole is almost 3000 metres above sea level). The katabatic rolls away from the South Pole in a doughnut-like formation before it becomes relatively warm and rolls back down, eventually reaching the South Pole again. These winds are constant – and notoriously brutal. We love the word *katabatic*! *Hoosh* is the name given to the fatty soup that Antarctic explorers of the Heroic Age (1895–1922) have traditionally eaten as their staple. At the beginning of each trip, the hoosh will usually contain mainly pemmican (dried lean beef pounded into a paste, mixed with melted fats and pressed into small blocks) and dry biscuits. Later, as the expedition wears on and the supplies run low, the hoosh would typically consist of water, seal meat and blubber, penguin and any other bits that might be available, including old pieces of leather or the sledging dogs. The dinner pot that night contained a fine katabatic hoosh of noodles, onion, minced beef, garlic, peas, oil and tomatoes.

All three of us are reasonably well read (and Peter especially so) on the Heroic Age of exploration in Antarctica, and have a particular interest in the expeditions led by Amundsen, Scott, Mawson and Shackleton. We discuss the problem that having two Jasons on the trip might pose in terms of clarity of communication. It is suggested that we adopt names of Antarctic explorers from the Heroic Age.

Sun setting behind Mt Nelse

Chapter 2

EXPLORERS OF
THE HEROIC AGE

For scientific leadership, give me Scott; for swift and efficient travel,
Amundsen; but when you are in a hopeless situation, when there seems
to be no way out, get on your knees and pray for Shackleton.

Sir Raymond Priestly

There are many extraordinary stories about the explorers of the Heroic Age. This is merely a
glimpse into the experiences of the three remarkable men whose names we adopted on our
own Antarctic expedition at 80 degrees south – one a famous leader, the other two expedition
members long forgotten.

Dr Xavier Mertz. Photographer: Unknown

DR XAVIER MERTZ

Dr Xavier Mertz was born in Basle, Switzerland, in 1883. He was a doctor of law and was a champion cross-country skier. In 1911 he joined the Australian Douglas Mawson on the Australian Antarctic Expedition, which set out to trek and scientifically map Antarctica from Oates Coast to the Queen Mary Coast. In November 1912, Mawson, Mertz and the third member of the team, the Englishman Belgrave Ninnis, set out from their base at King George V Land on dog sledges, carrying all of their supplies, in search of the magnetic South Pole. The weather was unbelievably poor. Mawson notes in his diary, 'the winds have a force so terrific as to eclipse anything previously known in the world', before famously adding, 'we have found the home of the blizzard. We have come to an accursed land.'

With the team over 300 miles from their base, disaster stuck when Ninnis, along with his sledge and dog team, disappeared into a crevasse, never to be seen again. Ninnis had been carrying the tent and the majority of the supplies. Mawson said to Mertz, 'We are in dire peril Xavier ... we are some 320 miles from the hut and we have been out now for five weeks. We have the barest resources to get us back. You know what we must do to stay alive.' Mertz replied, 'Yes, we shall have to eat the dogs.'

Mertz and Ninnis with a box of frozen penguins
Photographer: Unknown

Mertz and Ninnis establishing camp on the plateau
Photographer: Unknown

Belgrave Ninnis. Photographer: Unknown

Sir Douglas Mawson. Photographer: Unknown

As Mawson and Mertz pushed on to return to base, the conditions became more difficult for both men.

Mawson was in terrible pain, unable to see, with a bad attack of snow blindness – in both eyes. Mertz doctored him, applying a mixture of cocaine and zinc sulphate under his eyelids. In an hour Mawson could almost see out of one eye, just enough to see Mertz prepare our supper. Mertz made a Hoosh, normally a rich mixture of pemmican [dried meat], butter, biscuits and water. Which was now no thicker than a strong tea. The dog liver, like the rest of the meat, scorched and did not fry. They ate it with their fingers, finding the taste undesirable and repellent but were thankful that it was at least easy to chew.

The dogs had no such problems gulping down their comrades as Mawson and Mertz were forced to kill them for food. Mawson's diary describes how he 'cut up half the remaining carcass and fed it, with the offal and head, to the five, frantic animals. In minutes, nothing was left but a depression in the snow.' But the consumption of the dog meat was still difficult for the humans. Cutting into the carcass, Mawson noted how 'relieved' he was when the liver appeared. They scorched it on each side and so they could swallow it in chunks. It would not be known until after Mawson's death in 1958 that eating entire dog livers delivers what is essentially a massive overdose of vitamin A. With all the dog liver being eaten, both Mawson and Mertz would each consume more than 30 toxic doses of vitamin A as they struggled to survive on the frozen continent.

Mertz with an ice mask. Photographer: Unknown

L-R: Mertz, Ninnis and Murphy. Photographer: F. Hurley

Lennard Bickel in his 1977 account of their journey, *This Accursed Land*, notes:

> '… a moment, still, please!' He plucked at Mawson's left ear. His fingers lifted away a complete skin cast … Alarmed, Mawson fumbled his right ear – and again the spread of skin came away. Mertz took off his own wet helmet and inside the wool, strips of skin and small tufts of beard were attached; there were raw patches at his temples, and his hairline had receded. Mawson noted that his companion's once-luxuriant black moustache was patchy, ragged, that the cracks round the mouth, nose and eyes – which he had put down to wind and cold – were opening into red, raw fissures, deep, like razor cuts, and runny.

> Was this condition only on their heads? They released the bottoms of their pants, and over their boots, on to the snowy floor, fell a small stream of skin strips and loose hair. 'I think our bodies are starting to rot,' he told Mertz. 'It is lack of nutrient.' … Mertz's eyes were dark with returning presentiment. 'I have felt all the time,' he said gloomily, 'that the diet of dog does not agree with me.' …

Mertz with a dog team. Photographer: B. Ninnis

Mertz and Basilisk. Photographer: Unknown

The nights following Christmas were filled with the drudging toil of climbing out of the Ninnis Glacier. The struggle to reach the 3000-feet high plateau of ice on the Western side carved deeply into their reserves of strength, and on the third night they sorrowed at the loss of the last husky ...

When Ginger's head had boiled for 90-minutes, they lifted it, with the two impromptu wooden spoons, onto the lid of the cooker. Mawson ran a knife across the top of the skull for the demarcation line; Mertz closed his eyes and Mawson touched one side of the head and asked: 'Whose?' They took turns in gnawing their different sides, biting away the jaw muscles, lips, swallowing the eyelids and gulping down the eyeballs. With the wooden spoons they scooped out the contents of the skull – and then split the tongue, the thyroids, the brain into two servings ... [Mawson noted] 'Had a good breakfast from Ginger's skull – ate brains, thyroid and all.' ...

'Get on the sledge, Xavier. The way is downhill and we can go a little farther, and perhaps you'll feel like walking again.' Mertz resisted. There was some affront for him riding the sledge; but Mawson insisted, pushing him onto the load, making him lie down, covering him with the sleeping bags ...

The canvas harness cut into his shoulders ... He staggered as his feet slid on the wind-polished surfaces ... sudden slip, a broken leg, or ankle and they would face the end ... He covered two and a half miles this way. Then Mertz was calling out, in pain. Mawson managed to erect the tent and get him inside within an hour; then he heated a thick cocoa-and-dog stew which he pressed on Mertz with the name of 'beef tea.' The name deceived Mertz' mind and he drank the hot liquid; yet, his stomach soon rebelled and he vomited into the snow ... In his journal Mawson expressed his anxiety: 'Things are in a most serious state for both of us. If he cannot go on and make eight or ten miles a day in the next day or two, then we are both doomed.

'I could perhaps pull through – with the provisions at hand – but I cannot leave him. His heart seems to have gone. It is very hard on me; to be within 100 miles of the hut and in such a position is awful.'

Mawson woke from a troubled dreaming of food to find the prospect of travel a shattered hope. Mertz was in a dire state. His trousers were fouled from an attack of dysentery, his eyes were wild and rolling, and he talked and babbled incoherently; he sounded demented. Mawson set to work cleaning Mertz' soiled clothing and was shocked to see his legs, his groin, stripped clean of skin, red, raw, rippled with painful folds ... Mertz raged: 'Am I a man – or a dog? You think I have no courage because I cannot walk – but I show you, I show ...' He lifted his left hand; the little finger – yellowed from frostbite – was thrust into his mouth and Mawson watched in stupefied horror as Mertz crunched his teeth into the

Mertz sits with his ice axe on a coastal ice formation near Cape Pennison. Photographer: F. Hurley

Mertz leaving the hut. Photographer: F. Hurley

middle joint, savagely severing the skin, cartilege [sic] and sinew, tearing away with grimaces and groans ... then, in disdain, spitting the severed digit into the floor of the tent ...

At midnight Xavier Mertz lay in a coma ... He reached out to touch his companion – and Xavier Mertz was stiff, cold, quite lifeless under his hand.

Mawson was not travelling as poorly as Mertz but certainly had his problems. Unable to detect the cause of squelching in his boots, he removed them only to discover that his soles had become separated from the underside of his feet. He rubbed in some ointment and continued to plod on, Bickel records:

[Mawson noted that he was] '... in a terrible mess.' He was shocked afresh at his condition; a poor, desquamated, dessicated skeleton of a frame, from which the muscle tissue had vanished, wide patches raw with the friction of clothing and harness, inflamed in the groin, his black nails coming loose, his teeth shaky in their sockets, his jaws aching. And his hair! ... 'I have lost so much hair that I rival my reindeer sleeping bag, which is now moulting heavily. It is a race between us – who shall be bald first!'

Mawson somehow managed to return to base camp at Cape Dennison, Commonwealth Bay, and was met by a team who were waiting for any survivors to return before their ship, the *Aurora*, departed for the winter. The first question that this rescue team asked of Mawson was, 'My God. Which one are you?' Such was the appalling appearance he presented.

On his eventual rescue and return to Australia, Mawson was moved to quote from his favourite poet, Rudyard Kipling:

We bring no store of ingots,

Of spices or precious stones,

But we have gathered,

With sweat and aching bones.

Mertz was to have the Mertz Glacier and the undersea valley Mertz-Ninnis named in his honour.

Jason Veale will be known as Dr Xavier Mertz.

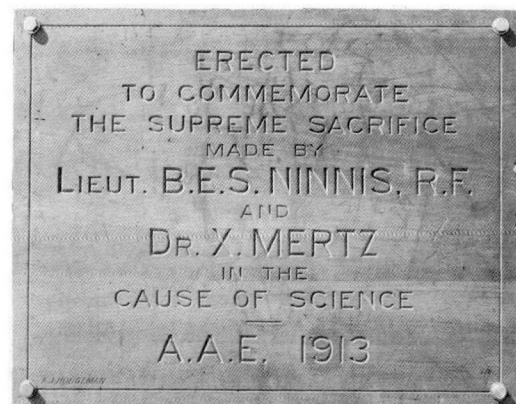

Inscription on the memorial cross, Cape Patterson. Photographer: F. Hurley

Sir Ernest Shackleton. Photographer: Unknown

SIR ERNEST SHACKLETON

After the conquest of the South Pole by Amundsen who, by a narrow margin of days only, was in advance of the British Expedition under Scott, there remained but one great main object of Antarctic journeyings – the crossing of the South Polar continent from sea to sea.

Sir Ernest Shackleton

Ernest Henry Shackleton was born in County Kildare, Ireland, on 15 February 1874. His family moved to London in 1884 to escape the last potato blight, and in 1890, at the age of 16 years, Shackleton went to sea, travelling to Africa, the East Indies and the USA. By 1896 he had been made first mate, and in 1898 he was promoted to the rank of master, qualifying him, at the age of 24 years, to command any British ship in any place in the world.

Shackleton, Scott and Wilson ready for their southern journey. Photographer: Unknown

The southern sledge party just returned. L–R: Shackleton, Scott and Wilson. Photographer: L. Bernacchi 1902

Shackleton was home on leave when he signed up to join Robert Falcon Scott on his 1901 National Antarctic Expedition aboard the *Discovery*. Shackleton suffered from scurvy on the trip and became so ill that he had to be evacuated aboard the relief ship *Morning*. While deeply disappointed, Shackleton had gained valuable insights into what it was to explore and survive on the frozen continent. He returned to England in June 1903 after recovering in New Zealand. On his arrival home, the Admiralty offered him the role of saviour, asking him to return to Antarctica and rescue Scott, who had wintered there for a second time and was thought to require help. But Shackleton did not accept this offer, preferring to make plans for his own expedition to the South Pole. In his own words, he wanted to 'prove himself a better man'.

Shackleton, known as 'the Boss' to his men, would not have to wait long for his next expedition south. In 1907 he was commissioned to lead the *Nimrod* Expedition. The expedition included the Australian Douglas Mawson, who would later lead his own expeditions to Antarctica, as well as Frank Wild (quartermaster), Alexander Macklin (surgeon), George Marston (artist)

Farthest south, January 1909. Photographer: Unknown

and Alfred Cheetham (third officer and boatswain), who would all later join Shackleton on his historic *Endurance* voyage of 1914–16. The *Nimrod* expedition was the first to reach the summit of Mount Erebus and made many valuable scientific observations about the conditions they experienced and the geography they saw. They even unloaded a motorised vehicle, which assisted with hauling loads to the first two food depots at 10 and 15 miles south of their departure point respectively.

After wintering in their newly built hut at Cape Royds, Shackleton took Wild, Jameson Marshall and Eric Adams south for the 1700-mile return trek to the pole. Edgeworth David led Mawson and Forbes Mackay on the 1250-mile return trek to the more accessible magnetic South Pole, which they completed successfully in February 1909. Shackleton and his South Pole crew were doing it tough. The ponies were not as useful as he had hoped but were a valuable food source for the depots that they left behind for the return trip.

Shackleton recovering aboard the *Nimrod*, 1909. Photographer: Unknown

On 26 November they beat Scott's 'furthest south' record, set in 1902. On Christmas Day 1908, the South Pole crew feasted on plum pudding, brandy, chocolate, a spoon of crème de menthe and cigars. By Shackleton's calculations, they had 250 miles to cover to reach the pole but only three weeks' worth of supplies. Shackleton's diary entry for 2 January 1909 notes, 'I cannot think of failure yet. I must look at the matter sensibly and consider the lives of those who are with me.' On 4 January 1909, however, he conceded that, 'The end is in sight. We can only go for three more days at the most, for we are weakening rapidly.'

The next three days saw them make slow progress into the face of gale-force katabatic winds; on the fourth day the men were unable to leave the tent. They turned back just 97 miles short of the South Pole. When they finally reached the first food depot on 13 February, they happily ate from one of the frozen horses, which 'tasted splendid'. On safely returning to England, Shackleton explained to his wife, 'I thought you would rather have a live ass that a dead lion.' He received his knighthood later that year.

Before long Shackleton was ready to go again. With the conquest of the South Pole by Amundsen and Scott, there remained one great challenge for Shackleton: 'the crossing of the South Polar continent from sea to sea.' To complete the land crossing, he would have to travel more than 1750 miles across unexplored territory. Twenty-eight men were picked from over 5000 applicants. When the funding for the expedition collapsed, Shackleton was forced to seek alternative funds, and benefactors included Sir James Caird, the British government and the Royal Geographic Society, as well as the Public Schools of England and Scotland, who helped purchase the dogs, which were in turn named after individual schools. As Shackleton was preparing the *Endurance* for the voyage, the dark shadow of war was cast over Europe. On the eve of his departure, Shackleton sent a telegram to the Admiralty, offering his ship for service. The reply came by return telegram: 'Proceed.' Shackleton, like many of his contemporaries, thought that the war would be over by Christmas.

On 8 August 1914, the *Endurance* sailed from Plymouth; the stated expedition goal was to sail to the Antarctic coast via the Weddell Sea before traversing the continent via the South Pole. They stopped at South Georgia Island to resupply and make final preparations for their expedition. As the ice began to close in, Shackleton wrote:

> As the pack ice gets closer the congested areas grow larger and the parts are jammed harder until it becomes 'closer pack' ... the opposing edges of heavy floes rear up in slow and almost silent conflict till high 'hedgerows' are formed round each part of the puzzle ... the drifting pack changes – grows by freezing, thickens by rafting and corrugates by pressure.

The *Endurance* frozen into the ice on mid-winter's day. Photographer: F. Hurley

The *Endurance* crushed by ice, October 1915. Photographer: F. Hurley

The *Endurance* became trapped, stuck fast in the pack ice within sight of land, in January 1915. Shackleton wrote, 'The *Endurance* was confined for the winter. The seals were disappearing and the birds were leaving us.' On 1 May, two months of total darkness began.

The ship and crew would remain locked in the drifting ice for nine months. On 27 October 1915, as the ice slowly began to crush the *Endurance*, Shackleton ordered that the crew abandon ship and salvage what they could from her. This new home on the pack ice would be known as 'Ocean Camp'. Frank Hurley, the Australian photographer, managed to save hundreds of glass-plate images that he had recorded of the expedition. He talked Shackleton into letting him keep 150 of his plates, but because of weight restrictions, the remainder, some 400 plates, were smashed so that Hurley would not be tempted to try to retrieve them later on. Hurley was also permitted to keep some of his camera equipment to record the rest of their journey. Shackleton realised that without the images they would have nothing but stories should they survive.

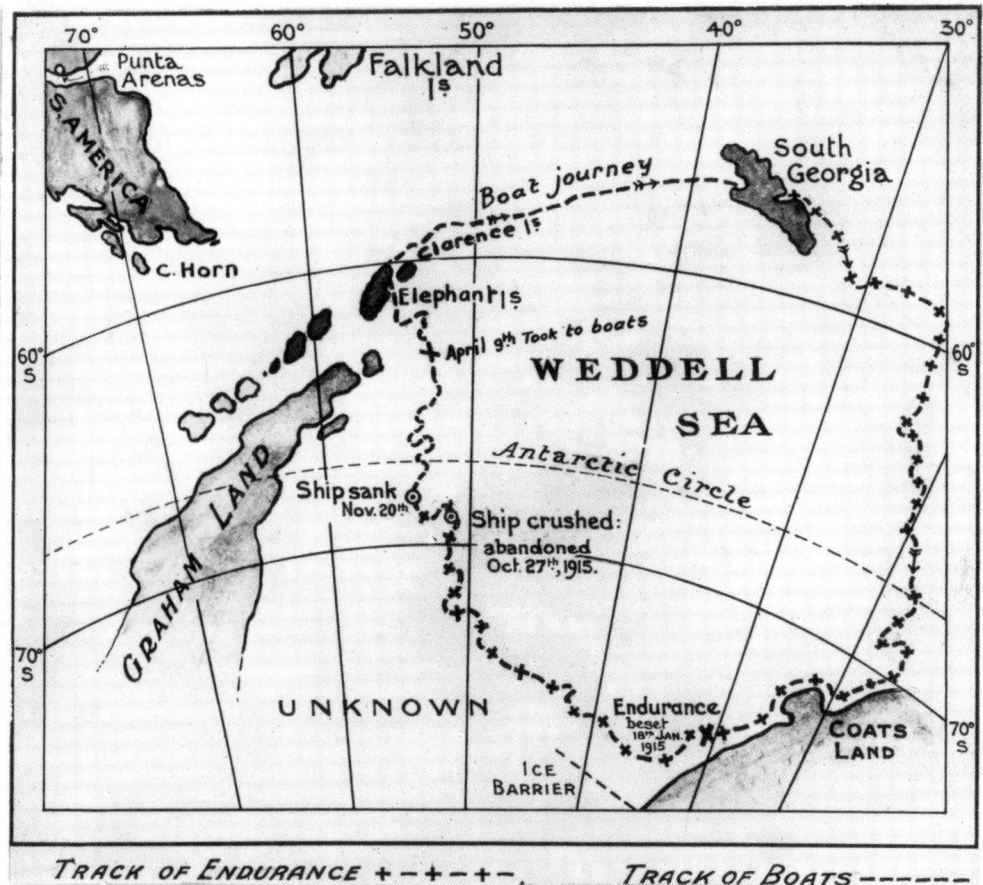

Route taken by the *Endurance* and her crew

The ship was reduced to kindling, finally sinking on 21 November 1915. Afterwards, Shackleton and his men lived for a further five months on the ice floes at Ocean Camp, Mark Time Camp and Patience Camp, drifting slowly north through the Weddell Sea towards the open ocean. The three smaller boats salvaged from the *Endurance* were named after their benefactors: *Dudley Docker*, *James Caird* and the *Stancomb-Wills*. The men survived on meagre rations that were supplemented with seal, penguin and any curious birds. The sledge dogs were killed and the young ones used for food. The diary of Harry McNeish records that, 'Their flesh tastes a treat ... after being so long on seal meat, and this last 14 days on almost nothing. We got 20 fish in the leopard [seal] stomach and we are having them for breakfast tomorrow.'

The pack ice eventually broke up on 9 April 1916, and after 156 days drifting on the ice floes, they loaded the boats and began the hazardous voyage to Elephant Island. The first night was spent camped on an iceberg, which split in two during the night, causing it to

Shackleton, Wild and the men at dump camp. Photographer: F. Hurley

be abandoned. The next five days were spent rowing on high alert in freezing conditions, avoiding icebergs and treacherous ocean currents that threatened to sweep them into oblivion. When Elephant Island was sighted, the men had to endure a further night on the water as an offshore current prevented them from making a direct approach. On 15 April, the three boats finally landed on Elephant Island. It was the first time that the men had stepped foot on solid land for almost a year and a half.

They spent several days on the island refitting the *James Caird* for the voyage to South Georgia Island. The remaining two boats were laid side by side atop a metre-high stonewall with their hulls facing skyward. Lashed together, they became home – known as 'the Snuggery' – for the men who remained on Elephant Island. Shackleton set off for South Georgia Island in search of rescue with Frank Worsley, McNeish, John Vincent, Timothy McCarthy and Tom Crean.

Green cooking in camp on sea ice. Photographer: F. Hurley

McNeish skinning penguin for the blubber stove, with Shackleton. Photographer: F. Hurley

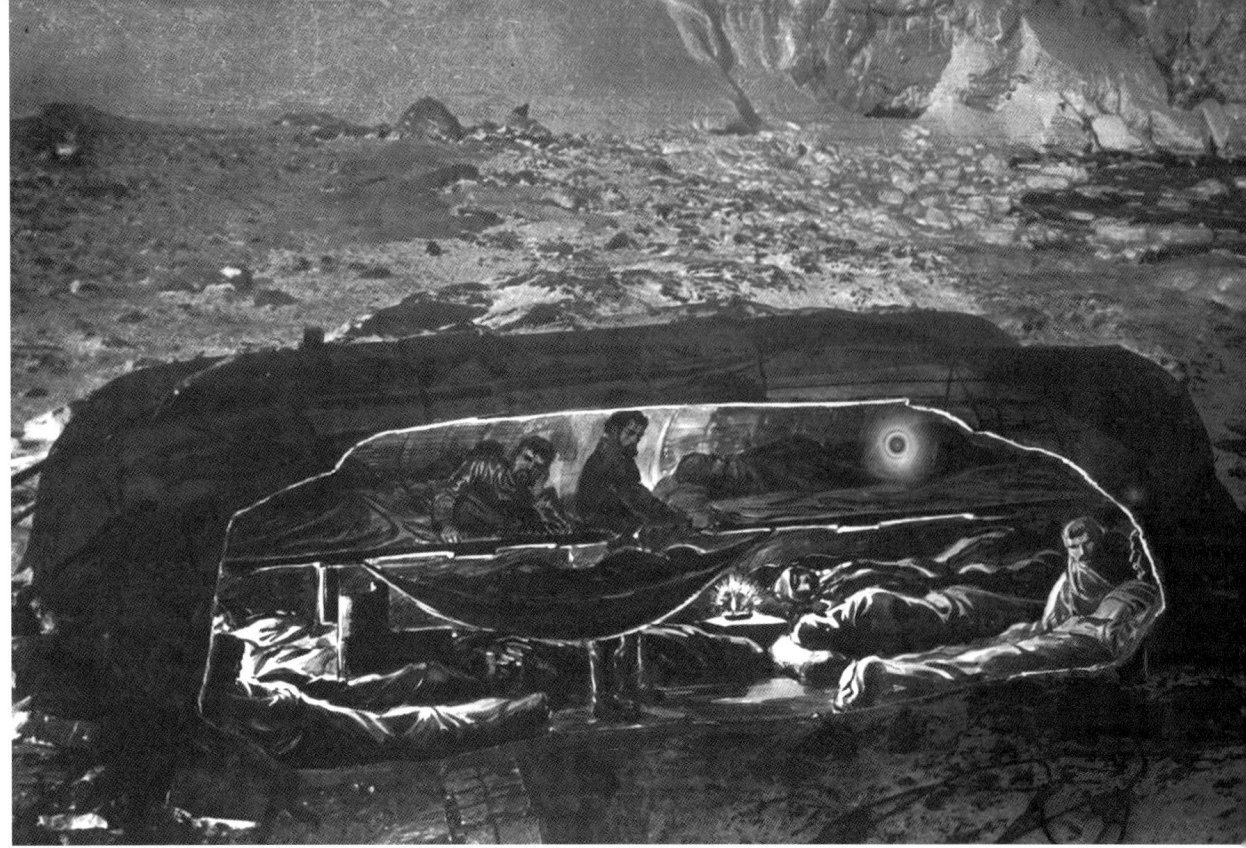

Cross section of the snuggery. Artist: Unknown

The monumental voyage to South Georgia Island would take Shackleton and his men across the most storm-swept, violently pitching ocean in the world. South Georgia Island was 860 miles from Elephant Island, and they would attempt the voyage in the converted lifeboat, the *James Caird*, which was not more than 23 feet long. Every day for the next 17 days, the boat was frozen over with ice, which then had to be broken off to prevent it from becoming sluggish and being swamped. The crew were tossed about on the waves in the freezing cold, their reindeer sleeping bags turned to sludge. They lived on the knife-edge, knowing that each moment could be their last. It is hard to imagine the shocking conditions they endured.

On arrival at South Georgia, Shackleton was unable to land at the Norwegian whaling station Grytviken as planned because of horrific winds. Instead he was forced to land at Haakon Bay on the other side of the island. In a remarkable feat of navigation, they had found their needle in the haystack. Shackleton determined that the only possible way to reach Grytviken was to traverse the island's previously unexplored mountain ranges with Worsley and Crean using only makeshift equipment. Remember that these men were seamen and polar explorers, not mountaineers.

The snuggery, Elephant Island. Photographer: F. Hurley

Launching the *James Caird* for the 1300km voyage to South Georgia, 24 April 1916. Photographer: F. Hurley

Grytviken Whaling Station. Photographer: F. Hurley

They eventually staggered into Grytviken Whaling Station at Stromness, 36 hours after landing at Haakon Bay. The men were unrecognisable, with heavy beards, large clumps of matted hair and sooty faces from their blubber stoves. The trek across South Georgia has been attempted many times since Shackleton blazed the trail, by fully-equipped and supplied teams of experienced climbers. As yet, no group has completed the journey in less than three days.

When they arrived, the three bedraggled men were taken to the manager of the whaling station, Mr Sorlle, whom Shackleton knew well from previous visits. On 20 May 1916, Shackleton wrote, 'Mr Sorlle came to his door and said, "Well?" "Don't you know me?" I said. "I know your voice," he replied doubtfully. "You're the mate of the Daisy." "My name is Shackleton," I said.' Sorlle let the men into his house as tears ran down his cheeks.

Shackleton's immediate concern was the rest of his men. Worsley took a boat to Haakon Bay to rescue Vincent, McNeish and McCarthy, whom he found huddled under the *James Caird*. Shackleton tried to reach his surviving men on Elephant Island first with the Norwegian whaler *Southern Sky*, which was forced back by pack ice only 60 miles short. He retreated to the Falkland Islands, where he loaned a trawler, *Instituto de Pesca*, from the Uruguayans, but again they were blocked by impassable ice.

South Georgia mountains. Photographer: F. Hurley

From here they returned to Punta Arenas, where funds were quickly raised for the charter of the *Emma*. The *Emma* was towed by the *Yelcho* to save the precious fuel, but on being cut free, the engine on the *Emma* failed just short of its final approach to Elephant Island. So the *Yelcho* was used again, unencumbered this time and on loan from the Chileans with a volunteer crew led by Luis Pardo. The rescue party finally made it to Elephant Island on 30 August 1916.

The crew of the *Endurance* had spent five months on the rocky beach huddled under the boats, not knowing the fate of their rescuers. Hurley complained in his diary, 'We are heartily sick of being compelled to kill every bird that comes ashore for food.' The men were in a terrible state. The stinking black soot from the blubber stove had been absorbed into their clothing and turned their skin black. Hurley described himself and his companions as 'the most motley and unkempt assemblage that ever was projected on plate.' Shackleton did not lose a man on the *Endurance* expedition. The crew was safely returned to Punta Arenas, where they were treated to a heroes' welcome. Here they recuperated before returning to England.

Shackleton with dignitaries at Punta Arenas. Photographer: F. Hurley

Shackleton's final journey south was his 1921–22 voyage on the *Quest*. Now 48 years old, he planned a grand circumnavigation of the Antarctic continent, with some of his old crew along for the expedition. But Shackleton was not himself. Alexander Macklin, the team's doctor, noted in his diary, 'There is something different in him this trip as compared with the last, which I do not understand.'

In Rio de Janeiro, Shackleton suffered a heart attack but refused treatment. Instead he chose to self-medicate with champagne and cigars. He died on arrival at South Georgia Island and his body was shipped back to England for burial. When his wife, Emily, heard of this, she ordered that the body be sent back and buried with the whalers on South Georgia. By this time Shackleton's body had reached the Uruguayan city of Montevideo. He was turned around and headed south once more; this time he would find his final peace.

The crew of the *Endurance* at Punta Arenas. Photographer: Unknown

Shackleton's grave on South Georgia is inscribed with a line from 'The Statue and the Bust' by Robert Browning: 'I hold that a man should strive to the uttermost for his life's set prize.' Shackleton had once said, 'I seemed to vow to myself that someday I would go to the region of the ice and snow and go on and on till I came to one of the poles of the Earth, the end of the axis upon which this great round ball turns.'

Peter Hillary will be Sir Ernest Shackleton – 'the Boss' to his men.

Lawrence Oates. Photographer: H. Ponting

LAWRENCE OATES

I may say that this is the greatest factor – the way in which the expedition is equipped – the way in which every difficulty is foreseen, and precautions taken for meeting or avoiding it. Victory awaits him who has everything in order – luck, people call it. Defeat is certain for him who has neglected to take the necessary precautions in time; this is called bad luck.

Roald Amundsen, *The South Pole*

Lawrence Edward Grace Oates was born on 17 March 1880 in Putney, London. He was also known as 'Soldier' because of his service during the Boer War in South Africa, where his name was mentioned in many dispatches in relation to his courage in battle. Oates was seriously wounded while fighting in 1901 but returned to the front before the end of the year. This injury left him with a slight limp.

The following year he was promoted to the rank of lieutenant and served in India, Ireland and Egypt before achieving the rank of captain in 1906. Oates' other moniker was 'Titus' – a reference to the English conspirator Titus Oates (1649–1705), the infamous ringleader of the 'Popish Plot'.

In 1910 Lawrence Oates applied to join Robert Falcon Scott's British expedition on the *Terra Nova* to Antarctica and then trek all the way to the South Pole. He was selected from over 8000 candidates. They were to become the first men in the world to reach the South Pole and return alive. Scott's stated aim was 'to reach the South Pole and secure for the British Empire the honour of that achievement'.

Amundsen – with his 97 Greenland Huskies, experienced skiers and well-researched equipment needs – learnt about survival in Antarctica from extensive time spent living with the Inuit in Canada's northern territories: 'The English have loudly and openly told the world that ski and dogs are unusable in these regions and that fur clothes are rubbish. We will see – we will see.'

Scott, on the other hand, insisted on man-hauling his sledges, limited the use of skis, placed particular emphasis on the scientific components of his expedition but lacked extensive practical knowledge of what equipment would be required to make a safe return trip to the South Pole:

> In my mind no journey ever made with dogs can approach the height of that fine conception which is realised when a party of men go forth and face hardships, dangers, and difficulties with their own unaided efforts, and by days and weeks of hard physical labour succeed in solving some problem of the great unknown. Surely in this case the conquest is more nobly and splendidly won.

Captain Robert Falcon Scott. Photographer: John Thomson

Captain Roald Amundsen. Photographer: Unknown

Oates' responsibility was to tend the 19 Siberian-bred ponies that had been shipped from Vladivostok to Lyttleton, New Zealand, via Japan and Australia. These ponies were to do the bulk of the early hauling, creating food depots for the outward and return trips. Also on board were 39 dogs. A huge payload was taken aboard the *Terra Nova*: 3 motor sledges, 460 tons of coal, 3 tons of ice, 162 sheep carcasses, 3 tons of beef, 5 tons of dog food and numerous pieces of scientific equipment. Oates had always argued for 45 tons of feed for the ponies, but Scott regarded this as excessive. Oates was forced to settle for less, but managed to sneak another 2 tons of feed on board without Scott's knowledge.

The wives of some of the crew came with them as far as New Zealand. Tensions developed between some of the women, resulting in a fracas at the time of the *Terra Nova*'s departure from Dunedin on 29 November 1910. Oates records that:

> Mrs Scott and Mrs Evans had a magnificent battle, they tell me it was a draw after 15 rounds. Mrs Wilson flung herself into the fight after the 10th round and there was more blood and hair flying about the hotel than you see in a Chicago slaughter-house in a month, the husbands got a bit of the backwash and there is a certain amount of coolness which I hope they won't bring into the hut with them, however it won't hurt me even if they do.

Bunk beds – Oates is in the middle. Photographer: H. Ponting

Meares and Oates at the blubber stove. Photographer: H. Ponting

After several months of setting up the hut and placing the depots, the expedition bunkered in for the winter at Cape Evans. The sun disappeared on 23 April and would not reappear until 23 August. During the darkness of winter, Edward Wilson led a group to Cape Crozier, and one of the men on this expedition, Aspley Cherry-Garrard, recounts this ordeal in the aptly named book *The Worst Journey in the World*. He summed up his experience thus: 'Polar exploration is at once the cleanest and most isolated way of having a bad time which has been devised.'

On 1 November 1911, a ten-man team departed Cape Evans for the South Pole. They encountered unseasonably strong winds and blizzards, causing the remaining seven ponies to founder in the deep snow. After three weeks, the first pony was shot; one week later another was shot, and then the remaining five ponies were shot, skinned and left at a food depot two days short of the Beardmore Glacier. Each man was now pulling over 200 pounds on his sledge. On 3 January 1912, Oates, Edgar Evans, Henry Bowers and Wilson were chosen by Scott to join him on the final push to the South Pole.

Captain Oates and his ponies in their stable. Photographer: H. Ponting

The *Terra Nova*. Photographer: H. Ponting

Onboard the *Terra Nova*. Photographer: H. Ponting

Pole party at the Norwegian Tent. L-R: Scott, Oates, Wilson and Evans. 18 January 1912. Photographer: H. Bowers

On 18 January 1912, they reached the South Pole only to find a tent belonging to the Norwegian Amundsen, who had reached the pole 35 days previously and had left them a note telling them of their defeat. The news was devastating. Wilson wrote of Amundsen having 'beaten us in so far as he has made a race of it. We have done what we came for all the same.' The men must have been shattered; supplies were low, and there was a sense of foreboding among the group. Scott wrote, 'All the day dreams must go; it will be a wearisome return.' Amundsen returned safely to his base at Framheim on 25 January 1912, the return trek to the pole having taken him and his men three months. He announced the successful completion of his journey to the world when he landed his boat, the *Fram*, at Hobart on 7 March 1912.

To look at the photographs taken of Captain Scott and his men at the South Pole is to look into faces of death. You can sense an awareness of impending doom. The men turned around on the same day and headed back. Scott said of the South Pole, 'Great God, this is an awful place.' By now Oates' old war wounds were flaring up, scurvy had set in, and he was suffering terrible frostbite. Oates continued to have confrontations with Scott over the expedition.

At the South Pole. L-R: Oates, Bowers, Scott, Wilson and Evans. 18 January 1912. Photographer: H. Bowers

Oates writes, 'Myself, I dislike Scott intensely and would chuck the whole thing if it were not that we are a British expedition ... [Scott] is not straight, it is himself first, the rest nowhere.' Conditions on the return trip were particularly harsh. Travel was often impossible, and the cold unremitting. Petty Officer Evans died on 17 February 1912. Temperatures fell to −50°c, and everything depended on the men waiting for a break in the weather to make a dash for the next food depot. If the weather did not ease, the men could not move – and they became weaker.

As conditions worsened, Oates' frostbite became more severe, and on 16 March 1912 he asked that he be left behind. Scott refused this request, and Oates battled on for another day.

The following is Scott's diary entry for 17 March 1912:

> Friday, March 16, or Saturday, 17 [1912]. Lost track of dates, but think the last is correct. Tragedy all down the line. At lunch, the day before yesterday, poor Titus Oates said he couldn't go on; he proposed we should leave him in his sleeping bag. That we could not do, and we induced him to come on, on the afternoon march. In spite of its awful nature for him he struggled on and we made a few miles. At night he was worse and we knew the end had come.

Sledge hauling in soft snow. Photographer: Unknown

Should this be found I want these facts recorded ... we can testify to his bravery. He has borne intense suffering for weeks without complaint, and to the very last was able and willing to discuss outside subjects. He did not – would not – give up hope till the very end ... He slept through the night before last hoping not to wake; but he woke in the morning – yesterday. It was blowing a blizzard. He said, 'I am just going outside and may be some time.' He went out into the blizzard and we have not seen him since ... we knew that poor Oates was walking to his death, but though we tried to dissuade him we knew it was the act of a brave man and an English gentleman. We all hope to meet the end with a similar spirit, and assuredly the end is not far.

Oates died on his 32nd birthday. Scott, Wilson and Bowers pushed on for the next food depot, which was the One Ton Depot. They were stopped in their tracks by a fierce blizzard 11 miles short on 29 March 1912. A rescue party later found their bodies. In his last diary entry, Scott wrote:

L-R: Wilson, Scott, Oates and Evans. Pole party leaving depot #3. Photographer: H. Bowers

For my own sake I do not regret this journey, which has shown that Englishmen can endure hardships, help one another, and meet death with as great a fortitude as ever in the past. We took risks, we knew we took them; things have come out against us, and therefore we have no cause for complaint, but bow to the will of providence, determined still to do our best to the last. Had we lived I should have had a tale to tell of the hardihood, endurance and courage of my companions which would have stirred the heart of every Englishman. These rough notes and our dead bodies must tell the tale, but surely, surely, a great rich country like ours will see that those who are dependent on us are properly provided for.

Oates' body was never found. The search party erected a cross near the place he was last seen, marked with the following inscription: 'Hereabouts died a very gallant gentleman, Captain L.E.G. Oates, of the Inniskilling Dragoons. In March 1912, returning from the South Pole, he walked willingly to his death in a blizzard, to try to save his comrades, beset by hardships.' Oates has a stretch of the Antarctic coastline – Oates Coast – named after him. The *Terra Nova* had discovered this coastline earlier on the expedition in February 1911.

I will be Titus Oates.

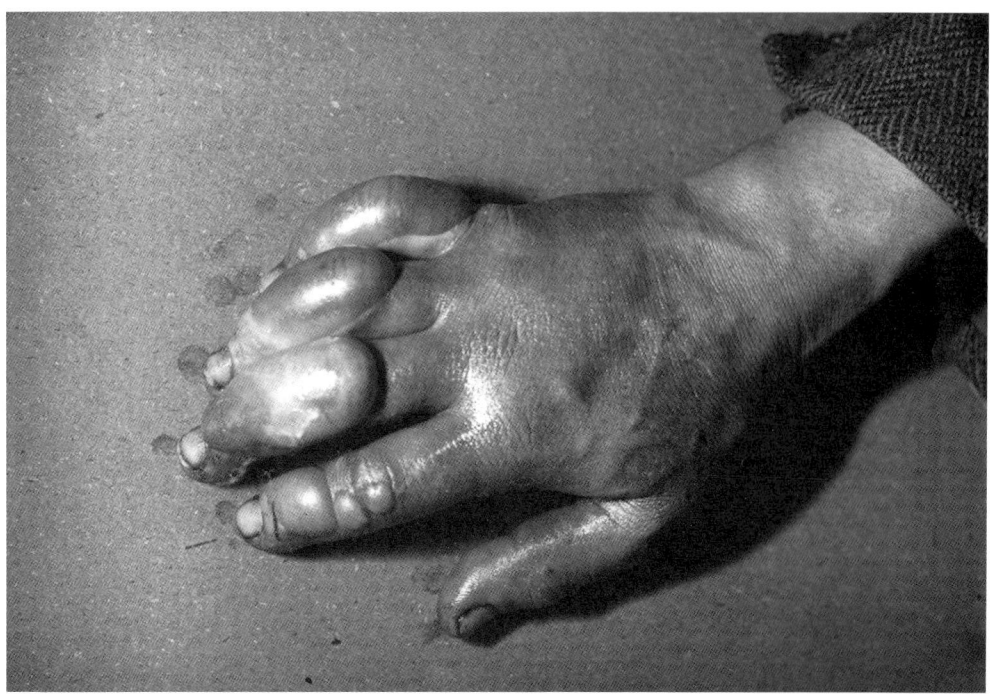

Frostbitten hand. Photographer: H. Ponting

One man's daily sledging food ration: cocoa, pemmican (dried meat), sugar, biscuits, butter and tea. Photographer: H. Ponting

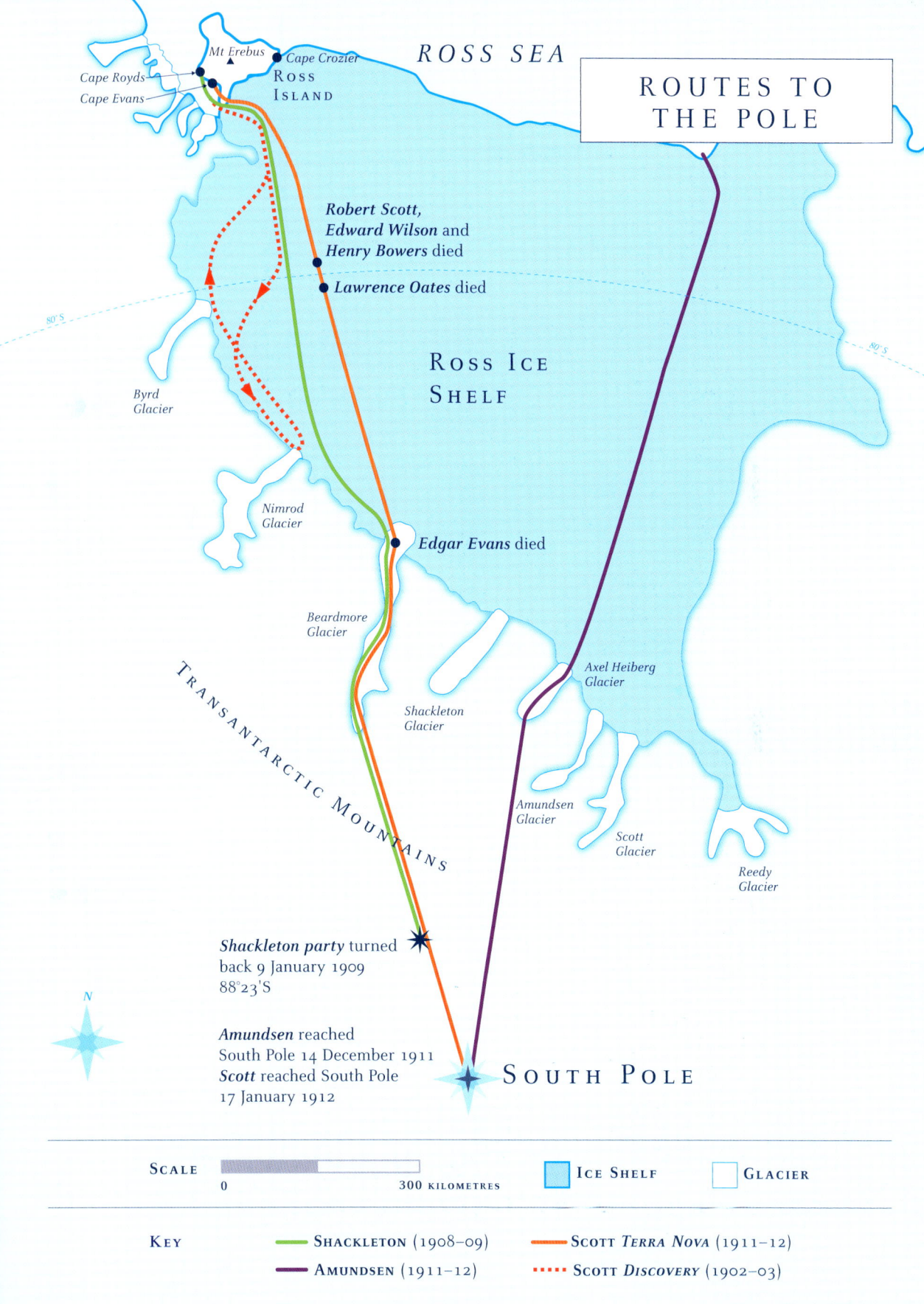

ROSS SEA

ROUTES TO
THE POLE

Mt Erebus ▲ Cape Crozier
ROSS
Cape Royds ISLAND
Cape Evans

Robert Scott,
Edward Wilson and
Henry Bowers died

Lawrence Oates died

80°S

Byrd
Glacier

ROSS ICE
SHELF

80°S

Nimrod
Glacier

Edgar Evans died

Beardmore
Glacier

Axel Heiberg
Glacier

Shackleton
Glacier

T R A N S A N T A R C T I C   M o u n t a i n s

Amundsen
Glacier

Scott
Glacier

Reedy
Glacier

Shackleton party turned
back 9 January 1909
88°23'S

N

Amundsen reached
South Pole 14 December 1911
Scott reached South Pole
17 January 1912

SOUTH POLE

SCALE   0   300 KILOMETRES   ICE SHELF   GLACIER

KEY   ——— SHACKLETON (1908–09)   ——— SCOTT *TERRA NOVA* (1911–12)
         ——— AMUNDSEN (1911–12)   ···· SCOTT *DISCOVERY* (1902–03)

Chapter 3

FINAL TRAINING CAMP: MOUNT RUAPEHU

It is late October, and there are only five weeks until our expedition departs. We have spent considerable time working on our gear and I am hopeful not to repeat my ill-prepared performance at Falls Creek. The next training location is Mount Ruapehu on the North Island of New Zealand, four hours out of Auckland, just beyond Lake Taupo.

Mertz and I fly to Auckland, where we are met by the Boss. We arrive at his home to be greeted by a full cooked breakfast prepared by Yvonne, the Boss's wife. The Boss shows us around his home before pausing in his office, where we all take a seat and begin to study various maps of Antarctica. The room is amazing, filled with photographs and curios from around the world, but there is one item that catches my eye. It is placed high on a shelf. Could it possibly be? I stand to full height and reach up for the object of my fascination. In my hand is a smallish box that, despite looking very old, remains in good condition. Printed on the side of the box is 'Hillary's Honey'. Of course! Ed Hillary, the Boss's father, was a bee keeper (an apiarist) before he became Sir Edmund Hillary, the first man to reach the summit of Mount Everest and the world's most famous mountaineer.

We load up the car and set off on our four-hour drive south. The Tongariro National Park, established in 1887, is the oldest in New Zealand and fourth oldest in the world. The local chief, Te Heuheu Tukino, gave the area to the people of New Zealand to be preserved in its natural state. As we wind our way up through the park, we pass through the most mysterious landscapes – lava fields and ancient beech forests – before we disappear into prehistoric podocarp forest, where you can easily imagine a dinosaur leaping out from the mist.

We pull over to get our expedition gear on, as strong winds and snow have been forecast for higher up the mountain. As we pull up at the car park in the village, the wind is blowing at 80 kilometres per hour and gusting at up to 140 kilometres per hour; it is snowing heavily. The Boss describes them as the most horrific conditions he has ever encountered in 40 years of coming here. We are suitably impressed. The process of hauling all our gear up to the ski lodge is problematic in that we are blown over very easily as we weave through the jagged rock formations. The trick is to stay low in whatever lee you can find, lest you get blown down and end up spearing yourself on the razor sharp rocks jutting up from the ground.

That night we lay all our gear out in the lodge's recreational room and go through it all again, with the Boss checking that every item is adequate for what lies ahead. The wind is positively howling by now, and the ski lifts have closed early. All our equipment is laid out for tomorrow's trek up Mount Ruapehu. We have all made recent purchases for the trip, and Mertz and I are showing them off proudly like schoolboys at 'Show and Tell', seeking approval and occasional commendation from the Boss.

Mertz presents his new boots, which he describes as 'Assa-lows', to the Boss for approval, to which the Boss replies, 'Oh, the A-Solos.' Mertz, who is desperately trying to sound more knowledgeable in all things mountaineering than he is, is noticeably taken aback: 'Bugger it, yes, yes of course, the A-Solos.' My bag, which is to be towed on the sledge, is brought out for show. It is a large, 110-litre capacity, rubberised duffle bag and completely waterproof. A more impressive bag you will not find. The Boss gives it a stamp of approval as I nod knowingly in the direction of Mertz, who ruefully makes a ticking motion with an imaginary pen in his hand, as if to indicate 'tick all boxes'.

This bag is no blessing, as it turns out. The group's equipment and food are split evenly as we pack, but to my horror there is gear left over. The only place for it seems to be inside my big bag. Talk about outsmarting myself! Oh well. How hard can it be? The big bag is jammed full of equipment. Equipment, equipment – there is always so much bloody equipment.

GUIDE TO EQUIPMENT

01

02

03

04

05

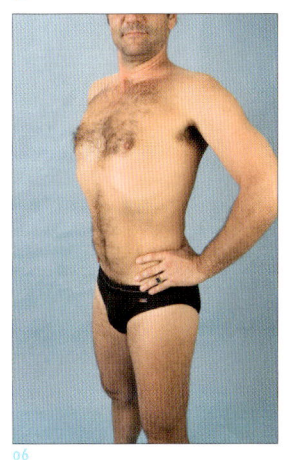
06

07

08

		QTY
01	Balaclava fleece and goggles	1
02	Down jacket with Gore-Tex outer shell	1
03	Polar fleece vest, fleece cap and sunglasses with crush-proof container	1
04	Polar fleece pants and jacket	1
05	Polypropylene tops and long johns	2 / 1
06	Polypropylene underpants	1
07	Sleep mask and beanie	1
08	Sun hat and head-dress, scarf for glacial glare and UV	1

GUIDE TO EQUIPMENT

09

10

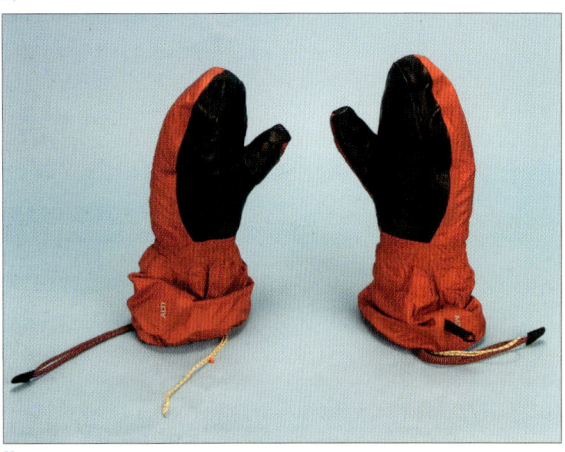

11

12

		QTY
09	Sleeping bag with Gore-Tex cover (–40°c)	1
10	Kit bag to be carried in sled	1
11	Gore-Tex mittens with Thinsulate lining (very warm) in a large size with wrist loop	**2 pairs**
12	Wool socks	**6 pairs**
13	Large pack with excellent harness and waist belt	1
14	Gaiters (important to check that they fit over ski mountaineering boots!)	**1 pair**
15	Pee bottle (1 litre)	1
16	Thermos with wide mouth (2 litre)	1
17	Foam mat and Therm-a-rest self-inflating mattress	1

13

14

15

16

17

18

19

20

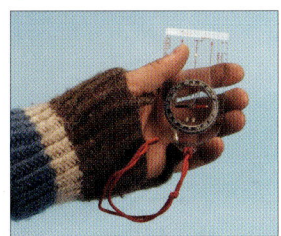

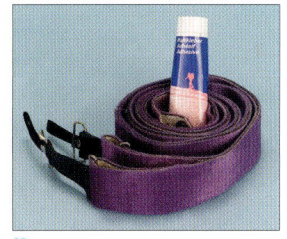

21

22

23

24

QTY

18	Ski mountaineering or mountaineering boots for cold climate (eg Scarpa or Koflach) and crampons with bindings	**1 pair**
19	Booties, large and warm, for tent and around camp (optional)	**1 pair**
20	Insulated bowl and mug, plastic spoon and fork	**1 each**
21	Hand pump for sleeping mat (moist air from lungs will freeze inside sleeping mat)	**1**
22	Compass	**1**
23	Skins and glue for skis (sticky base with heal tension strap)	**1 pair**
24	Gas lighter and polypropylene gloves	**1 / 1 pair**

GUIDE TO EQUIPMENT

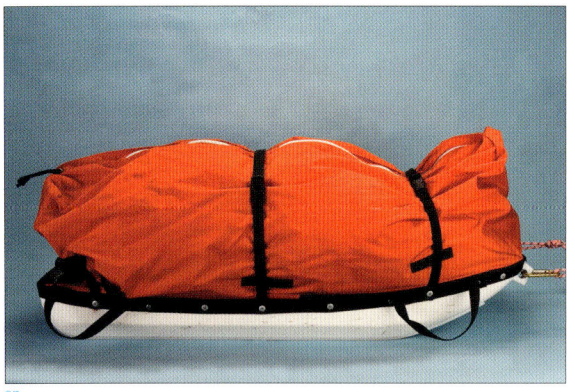
25

26

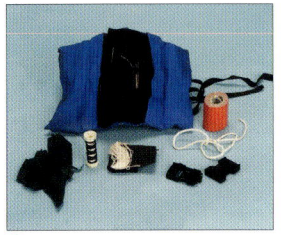
27

28

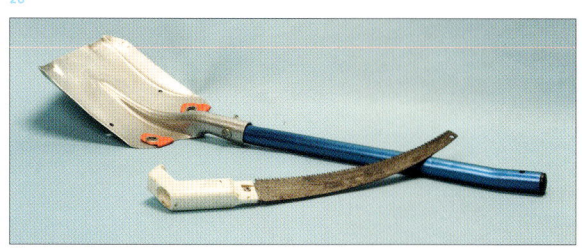
29

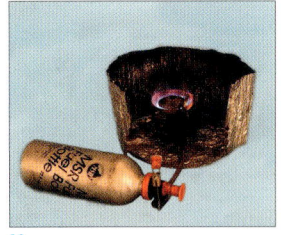
30

31

32

33

		QTY
25	Sled and 15 metres of 5-millimetre cord	1
26	Chefsway freeze-dried meals	60
27	Sewing kit, including needles, threads and spare clips	1
28	Cooking pots, serving spoon and ladle	2 / 1
29	Snow shovel and snow saw	1
30	MSR stove, insulated stove base and fuel bottle	1
31	Camera gear (optional)	1

34

35

36

37

38

		QTY
32	50-metre 8–9-millimetre rope (one for team)	1
33	Stuff sacks	3
34	Ski poles (with self-arrest handles, optional) and harness	1 pair
35	Snow stake	1
36	Satellite phone (as required by ALE for scheduled daily calls)	1
37	Fold-out seat with back support	1
38	Mountaineering skis, ski mountaineering bindings, hooded Gore-Tex jacket and over-pants	1 pair each

GUIDE TO EQUIPMENT

39

40

41

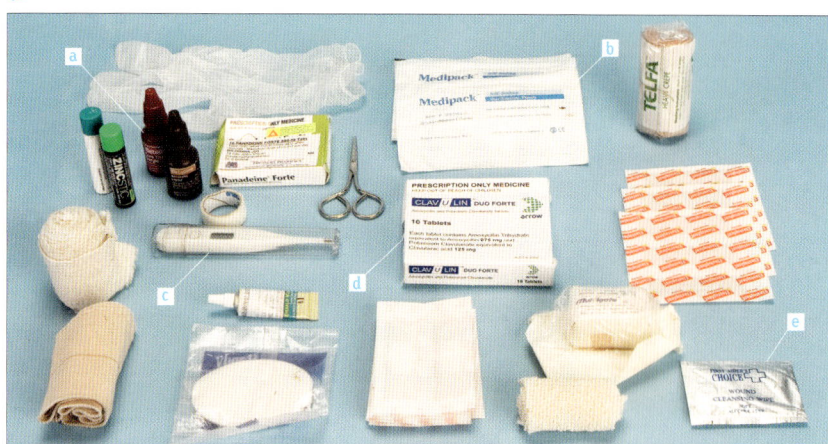

42

		QTY
39	Ice axe	1
40a	Prussics	**1 pair**
40b	Ice screws	**4**
40c	Slings	2
40d	Figure-8 descender	1
40e	Carabiners	**6**
40f	Screw gate carabiner	1
41	Petzel ascenders	2
42a	Medical kit, including antiseptic	1
42b	Sterile gauze	2
42c	Thermometer	1
42d	Antibiotics	1
42e	Swab	2

We prepare our sledges carefully, together, and ensure that the weight is evenly distributed so as not to repeat the debacle at Falls Creek. We attach the skins to the underside of our skis to ensure a good grip on the snow as we ascend Mount Ruapehu. The skin grips the snow so you can ski up a gentle incline without sliding backwards. I notice that my skins do not cover the width of my new skis – there is about 1 centimetre of exposed ski on either side of the skin. I am slightly concerned, but the Boss reassures me that it should be fine – note *should*, not *will*!

The next day the weather lifts and the sunshine breaks through; it is hard to believe that we are in the same place. So we head for the chairlift – which by the way is the best and most highly recommended way of getting to the summit of any mountain – with all of our gear. The ground is bereft of any snow, making the towing of sledges impossible. We are forced to carry the sledges and backpacks and skis. We arrive at chairlift one with the gear just in time for it to brake down. Umm, bad omen for the day. So we haul off to the nearby chairlift two, which is a further 100 metres uphill. It works. Our bags are loaded onto the chairs as they pass, and we follow the bags up. Wow, this is the way to climb a mountain. Look at the magnificent vista. Check out the valley below. Enjoy this as much as you can, I am thinking, because nothing lasts forever ... 'Get off!' yells the lift attendant. Geez, I forget to alight at the top of the lift and make a late jump.

We connect with another chairlift, which takes us to the highest point on the mountain that is accessible by chairlift. By now the sun is hot on our backs, and the snow is very sloppy under our skis. The Boss points out where we are headed. Mertz and I confirm the direction: yes, that's right, straight up!

I have never been up this steep a gradient covered with soft snow – and those damned skins do not cover the entire underside of the ski. Will this be a problem? The first few hundred metres are a total struggle. There is something wrong. I look down and see that I have neglected to unlock my heels from the ski bindings. Things become instantly easier when I release the heel lock, allowing my feet and legs to move freely. It is getting very hot and I am sweating like a horse. By now the incline has become what I will call 'challenging'. Forty minutes later it is extremely difficult. It is a stifling 10°c and I have stripped down to a light jacket and pants. Oh well, I think, it won't be this steep in Antarctica. But this is of little help to me now; this mountain needs to be climbed.

So here I am again, last in the group, with Mertz and the Boss out of sight as they blast up the slope, leaving me with my 20-kilogram backpack, 40-kilogram sledge, skis with inadequate skin coverage for this steep incline, sunglasses that are fogging up continually, sun burning my neck, sweat pouring from me ... It is Falls Creek revisited! The only good thing is that it is not dark. But it will be soon if I cannot find a solution quickly.

Oh the horror! My greatest fear has been realised: I have reached the point at which my skis will not grip sufficiently to allow me to take my next step forward. I cannot go up, cannot go down. I need to find a new way to get up this particularly steep section. The Boss comes into view briefly; he is a long way up and is the size of an ant. At least I know what direction to follow. Mertz is nowhere to be seen.

I must now remove my skis without being pulled down the mountain by the sledge, which is constantly urging me down the slope. I haul the sledge to my side and wedge it in a hollow that I have dug in the snow. I remove the skis and strap them onto the sledge. The snow is very soft, and I sink to my waist. This will be tough! Trying to tread gently and avoid falling through the sunbaked snow, I edge up the mountain one step at a time.

Low cloud and mist begin to close in around me. The sweat turns cold on my skin and clothing. After a few steps I find a ridge in the soft snow, and now I sink only to my knees – not great, but better. My path ahead is straight up. If I am to trek sideways, the sledge will roll upside down and become impossible to pull up this steep slope. It is a matter of taking one step forward and slipping half a step back on the soft snow. I approach some shaded snow, anticipating a harder surface – this is helpful, and my steps are surer.

It takes me over an hour to cover 200 vertical metres before the slope flattens a little allowing me to reattach the skis. With skis back on and the terrain relatively flatter, progress is good, and within an hour and a half I reach the final campsite for the day, at 2515 metres. I am exhausted and collapse in the snow for a few moments to gather my thoughts over a big drink of water. It is now very clear to me that my performances are just horrible on the first day of any alpine trek. Tomorrow is another day.

We dig the tent into a ledge on the mountainside with a snow wall all the way around the windward side. This takes over an hour to build. The sun is setting in the west over the Tasman Sea, casting a beautiful soft glowing light over the mountain and turning the snow from white to gold. We warm ourselves around the stove in the tent as I cook up a katabatic hoosh of mince, onions, herbs, bay leaves, corn, carrot and tomatoes. We all tuck in for an early night in preparation for a big day tomorrow.

Volcano lip

Perched on the volcano lip with a sulphuric acid lake below. Photographer: P. Hillary

We are rudely woken at 6 a.m. by the roaring stove as the Boss boils the water pot for a breakfast brew. We break camp at 8 a.m. and set off for the summit of Mount Ruapehu with our tent still in the shade. It is a rather cool –10°c degrees. The summit stands at 2800 metres and forms the rim of an acid lake, which has erupted as recently as 1996, when it spewed steam, sulphur and ash over the Tongariro National Park. We assure each other that we would be desperately unlucky to experience an eruption as we climb to the summit.

Carrying only a light backpack each with snacks, water and ropes for our half-day trip, we leave our camp on the ledge and shuffle up and over the first hummock, where we see the summit for the first time – a classic cone-shaped volcanic rim with the summit of Mount Ruapehu peaking out directly ahead of us. The sulphuric acid lake looms before us as we edge along the rim of the cone for the long climb to the top.

Rim of volcano

Lip of volcano

As we move along the lip of the cone, the path ahead becomes steeper, narrower and decidedly more challenging. The lip is only a metre or two wide and is covered in snow, ice and loose rocks. To our left is a 500-metre drop into the lake of sulphuric acid (it sounds nasty, I don't know what would happen if you fell in – probably just drown under the weight of all your equipment). To our right is a particularly steep drop of 2000 metres over volcanic rock and ice to farmland on the valley floor. At this stage I am unroped, leading the group along the rim and absolutely loving it. There is danger, there is excitement, and there is a real challenge in rock-hopping along the narrow rim. I am using the crampons and ice axe to great effect and feeling as confident as a mountain goat – and probably smelling a little like one too.

Push to the summit. Photographer: P.Hillary

Off in my own world, I am feeling as good as I can remember ever feeling on a mountainside, taking in the views, but never looking directly down, and scrambling over all the crags and ledges with delight. Just as I am about to burst with glee, I hear a distressed voice from behind calling on me to wait. We have all agreed as a group that if one of us were ever to become uncomfortable with the situation, he will speak up and express his concerns to the others. It's Mertz: 'Guys, I am feeling a bit jittery and just thought that it was time to tell you both that I will not proceed any further without a rope.' When asked about the source of his jitters, Mertz replies: 'Well, to my left is a very steep drop into a lake of sulphuric acid. To my right is a neverending slide into a farmer's paddock. Did I mention that I am essentially walking on a narrow plank of icy, crumbling, windswept rock? Am I clear?' Very clear, Mertz. We attach

Atop the summit

Roped traverse

Afternoon ski

Returning to camp

Mertz to a fixed rope and belay him along the remainder of the volcanic rim. The wind picks up while we wait in the shade as the Boss goes ahead with the rope. The temperature drops to −15°c, and we cool down quickly on the exposed ledge. A dull cold sets in.

After an hour, we are able to move into the sunshine, and we start to thaw out a little. Another hour sees us on the summit, where we meet another climber who has ascended from the other side, which is fortuitous as he is able to take a photograph of us. From the top we can see the Tasman Sea, approximately 60 kilometres to the west, and the Pacific Ocean, almost 65 kilometres to the east as the landscape fades into the great ocean. It is not often that you get to see both sides of a country at the same time. It is quite a thrill.

After sucking in the thin, cold air and surveying other peaks in the area, we decide to return to camp via the direct route along the edge of the sulphuric acid lake. This will involve reversing down the steep slope of the volcanic rim and using our ice axes and crampons to secure our descent. We manage this successfully and then take an hour off to enjoy some hot drinks, a snack and a good lie down on the sun-bathed snow. The temperature has risen from −15°c an hour and a half ago to +16°c degrees in the sun and out of the wind. Life in the mountains is never predictable and they certainly command respect.

Sunset from our tent

After spending the afternoon doing some rope work and preparing for dinner, we have another early night. Rising at 5 a.m. the next day, we climb the other major summit on the volcanic rim before sunrise, arriving at the top as the sun comes up just after 6 a.m. The views are absolutely stunning, with light, wispy clouds catching the first light of the day and steam billowing out of the sulphuric acid lake below.

As we return to camp, Mertz stops to practise his self-arrest technique with his ice axe. If you should happen to fall with your ice axe when trekking across a steep slope, the idea is to grab the ice axe handle with your left hand at your left hip while your right hand holds the axe end hard against your right shoulder, with the pick facing away from you and towards the slope. Mertz, keen to show off his newfound skill, leaps off the slope and hits the ground extremely hard, landing on his chest. Consequently he is a little slow in planting the axe head into the slope to self-arrest. Having knocked the wind out of his owns sails, dear old Mertz lies motionless on the slope, gasping for the air that is reluctant to come – much to the amusement of the Boss and myself. Mertz eventually recovers and does a great job of leading us down to the high camp.

We pack up and look forward to the trip back down. Surely it has to be easier than the journey up. We lock down our bindings so that we can downhill ski to the village below. The only problem is that we are still carrying backpacks and towing sledges, which are intimidating beasts when moving downhill. They have a nasty habit of getting up considerable speed, overtaking you, ripping at your hips and spinning you around before dumping you onto the hard snow.

The snow has developed a frozen crust overnight but is soft and uneven underneath, making for very difficult skiing. I decide that there is only one thing for it, and that is to go as fast as possible before losing control and crashing at high speed – spectacular and entertaining for the Boss and Mertz; fast, painful and exhilarating for me. Having survived more than 30 falls in the space of an hour, I limp into the kiosk for a cup of tea. The bruising is sensational. Large patches of purple and blue cover my hips and thighs. Mertz and the Boss join me some time later, having taken the more sensible approach of removing their skis and walking their sledges down the mountain.

At the bottom we all pile into the car and return to Auckland. Mertz and I are to fly back to Australia while the Boss says a quick hello and goodbye to his family. He is off to the USA for a ten-day lecture tour for corporate heavyweights. The Boss is a very busy man.

Lunch break at the acid lake. Photographer: P. Hillary

The Boss on the acid lake shore

Chapter 4

PUNTA ARENAS

Friday, 25 November comes around very quickly. When you are preparing to go away for a month, you are in such a frenzy for the two weeks prior to departure that you wonder at times whether it is worth going at all. Well, you don't ever *really* think that, but you do get incredibly busy in those last two weeks.

At the airport there are teary goodbyes from my mother, Connie, and my wife, Caroline, but young Florence (who is almost one and a half years old) and I manage to keep it together. In the lounge I meet up with a couple of mates, Mike Nicholls and Mitch McAuley, who are heading to South Georgia Island via the Falklands to do some painting. We all get chatting and miss our boarding call, so we dash to the gate and just make the flight.

When we finally get on the plane, a sense of comfort and relaxation washes over me. The newspaper can be read; food can be eaten without my delightful daughter using it for paint (and me for her canvas) in her latest artwork. I appreciate the elbowroom, even if this appreciation only lasts a few minutes – OK, maybe an hour – before I start to miss the mess.

My arrival at New Zealand goes smoothly, and I am very happy to see Mertz and the Boss in sparkling form. What a pleasure to be travelling with these men. We pass the time with a few laughs, and before long we are lining up for boarding at the departure gate. My name is announced and I am asked to report to the counter. Mertz and the Boss jokingly suggest that there has been a double booking and that my ticket is invalid. As I approach, the young lady smiles and takes my ticket: 'You have been upgraded, Mr Kimberley.' Wow! This is unheard of. The trip has taken on a new dimension.

The flight is a breeze – a seat that fully reclines, great food, and movies on demand. The only interruption is several sorties into the galley to steal some extra supplies for Mertz, who is very hungry on his meagre rations down the back. There are some delays in Auckland and head winds all the way over, so we arrive into Santiago, Chile, an hour late. It is midday.

We miss our connecting flight to Punta Arenas but find a hotel near the airport, check in and go for a swim. A taxi tour of Santiago and a few beers over a late lunch are a perfect way to spend the rest of the day.

We are up early the next day for our flight to Punta Arenas. The flight is uneventful, but the arrival is not. What is it with uniformed South Americans and their obsession with stamping passports and endless officialdom? We disembark from our domestic flight and pass several uniformed men at a desk – with impressive big stamps and ink pads at hand. We are called back to the desk to be met with the familiar mantra, 'Passports! Passports!' We explain that we have just arrived from Santiago and, as this is a domestic flight, unfortunately you guys don't get to stamp our passport this time. This falls on deaf ears. These stamp and ink fanatics insist on stamping our passports despite repeated explanations that we have come directly from Santiago. What would we know? Welcome to Punta Arenas, the southernmost town in the world.

Punta, as we come to know it, is situated on the Magellan Straits, which were discovered by the Portuguese explorer Ferdinand Magellan in 1520. Magellan had been looking for a passage west through the archipelago of Terra Del Fuego to avoid going around Cape Horn

Street scape, Punta Arenas

and risking all on his circumnavigation of the globe. He was the first European to see this great calm ocean, and he named it the Pacific. Sadly, Magellan never made it home to receive a hero's welcome, instead being speared to death by fractious tribesmen in the Philippines. Of the 250 crew members and five ships that set out in 1519, only eighteen men made it back on one ship. The discovery of the Magellan Straits meant that shipping vessels no longer had to tackle the treacherous seas of Cape Horn, instead taking the relatively safe route through the straits, passing directly by Punta Arenas.

Spanish colonists followed soon after and began to farm in the area. Sheep and cattle thrived there, as deep-sea fishing also took off; in fact, Punta was a boomtown in the late nineteenth and early twentieth centuries. There was a fishing fleet, a large pier, railway yards, a tugboat fleet, cattle yards and shipyards, and Punta did roaring business as a service and supply town for the passing ships.

Many mansions and impressive buildings were built at that time, largely financed by the global wool boom. But with every great boom must come the bust, and it came quickly. When the Panama Canal opened in 1914, enabling all shipping to take a significant short cut, Punta ceased to have any relevance and promptly collapsed. This gets me thinking: what was the plan for Punta once the Panama Canal opened? Did the local business leaders just pretend it wasn't happening? It wasn't as if they didn't know about the construction of the canal. My research comes up with nothing. Perhaps they are still in denial.

Punta's glory days have vanished long before we arrive. It is a desolate, windswept, rubbish dump – literally, with loads of rubbish dumped in and around the town. It is the kind of place that you would only visit if you had to – on the way to somewhere else. The population is 120 000, and the main industry seems to be the servicing of a massive prison behind the hill on which the town is situated. The prison is neatly tucked away and would have to be one of the largest ever built. It seems to go on forever – well, for at least 2 kilometres. We make some enquires around town about the prison and its location, and everyone we ask tells us of the futility of escape. If a prisoner were to escape, the available options are: swim for it in the icy waters; traverse the impassable Patagonian Desert; or take your chances crossing into Argentina and evading the border guards. There is no escape, even if you manage to get yourself out of the prison.

Nor do you come to Punta for the climate, with an average maximum of 6°c and winds averaging 20–25 knots during summer and spring; winter doesn't bear thinking about. The town's travel brochure notes, however, that, 'As the best and largest port for thousands of kilometres, Punta Arenas attracts ships from the burgeoning South Atlantic fishing industry as well as Antarctic research and tourist vessels.' Never mind that Ushuaia (just across the straits in Argentina) is the current boomtown, with lucrative government tax breaks for all business and trading. It just depends how you look at it.

Political billboards

The day after our arrival, we head off to a briefing session from Antarctic Logistic Expeditions (ALE), the logistics operator that will be flying us south to Patriot Hills. It is all rather boring really, but we do get to meet the other teams who are to join us on our flight south. There is a team of three Brits who are going to climb Mount Vinson with their guide, who has spent the past twenty years guiding in Pakistan. We ask him what it is about climbing in Antarctica that sets it apart from other parts of the world. His response sticks with me: 'Oh, it's the cold, it's the co-o-o ...' He tapers off, unable to finish his sentence as he stares vacantly into the distance. Another group of five very funny Brits and one Icelander (Andrew, Andrew, Andrew, Jason, Richard and Gunnie) are attempting to drive their converted Ford van to the South Pole. Gunnie, the Icelander, is the team's mechanic and driver. There is also Dianne, who skied to the South Pole recently, and her client, a radiologist from the USA. And three scientists are undertaking a research trip to try to prove the existence of unbelievably small space particles that are thought to pass through the Earth. Apart from the flight down, this will be the only time we are all together.

Every day we go on extended walks around Punta. A national election campaign is in full swing, and the streets are filled with banners supporting the various candidates. The most popular form of promotion is the large billboards with a big smiling mug shot of a smug candidate – usually a middle-aged or older man. Sometimes there are several men on the one billboard – it is unclear whether this is a symbol of unity or simple cost-cutting. We have heard that there is a female candidate, Michelle Bachelet, running for president, but she does not feature on any of the posters or huge billboards around Punta. She doesn't

seem to be very popular with the locals if prominence on billboards is any indication. Locals gather on street corners in the afternoon to wave yellow flags in support of the incumbent government. We will find out on our return that Michelle Bachelet has been elected the first female president of Chile.

Now we just have to wait until the weather clears at the landing strip in Antarctica so that we can take off. Sounds simple enough really. The landing strip is a 3200-metre blue ice runway that occurs naturally along the edge of the Patriot Hills at 80 degrees south. It is constantly being covered with snow blown in by the katabatic winds. This snow has to be removed by more wind (unreliable) or by the snow-blowing machines at the strip (very slow). There is also the problem of wind at Patriot Hills. The Russian pilots of our aircraft are reluctant to land in winds stronger than 15 knots because of the uneven landing surface and the isolated location. The cloud cover is a problem too, as are fog and spindrift – these are the tiny particles of snow and ice that are continually blown about by the wind, giving the impression that it is snowing even when it is not. So all the planets need to line up for a successful landing and subsequent take-off at Patriot Hills. We are on standby, ready to go at any moment. There are five scheduled phone calls to our hotel daily, advising us on the latest weather developments and the likelihood of departure.

All our trekking gear for Antarctica is carefully weighed and labelled before being loaded onto the Ilyushin, the four-engine Russian jet that will take us on the final leg of our journey south. This leaves us with only a few civilian clothes. We wait in our hotel room together while we catch up on some sleep. Then we wake up and wait some more.

The bloody weather! The Russian pilots are waiting for perfectly still and stable conditions, with no wind gusts, in which to land. They also need clear skies. There is a communications tent at Patriot Hills where all weather news is relayed back to Punta. These weather reports determine whether we go or not. We could be called to fly at any hour, so we cannot stray far from Punta lest we miss the scheduled phone calls. The weather updates are always tedious, very boring and offer little hope of departure.

WEATHER UPDATE ❋❋❋

Blowing snow reduces visibility to 10 metres. Wind blowing 33 knots gusting 52 knots. Absolutely horrific conditions in camp. Wind making it impossible to do anything. Wind 31 knots gusting 33 knots. We are getting hammered by wind. Wind 30 knots gusting 40 knots. Runway workable but drifting in. Some high wind speeds recorded. Winds picked up noticeably since last reading. No fly day. ❋❋❋

The wait for the weather to clear isn't so bad. How long can it take? Deciding to embrace the local culture, we set off for a restaurant that has been recommended by the hotel. We arrive at Los Ganaderos and embrace the culture via the local beer. The waiters are all in traditional gaucho outfits, and the centrepiece of the establishment consists of several lamb carcasses splayed open on metal racks and strategically placed around a roaring fire. For meat eaters, this is a very impressive sight. After a side of lamb each, washed down with several local beers, we all feel very cultured.

As we wander the streets, we come across the town square, which features the only patch of green grass in town and a statue of Magellan at its centre. At Magellan's foot, on the base of the statue, are two statues of indigenous natives. The locals say that those who 'kiss the big toe of the native' are destined to return to Punta Arenas. Although we are not particularly superstitious, we do not want to anger the local gods. Nor, however, do we particularly want to kiss the big toe, which on closer inspection appears to be covered with someone else's fresh saliva. We settle on a vigorous rub of the big toe. This is to become part of our daily ritual.

Over the next few days we work our way through the fine dining establishments and various nosh houses of Punta. Lomits, despite rhyming with 'vomits', is popular for a snack or lunch and is not as smoky as some places. Smoking in areas set aside for dining is very popular in Chile. The Hotel José Nogueira serves as good a meal as you could expect to find anywhere. The lamb cutlets are magnificent, as is the crab soup, and they are all served under a spectacular glass atrium.

We have eaten in what seems like every restaurant in town when the manager of our hotel, the Finis Terrae, invites us to 'Enjoy a delicious welcome drink in our sixth-floor restaurant'. Not wanting to be rude by pointing out that we have been his guests for some three days now, we take up the offer and head upstairs for an early dinner. Spectacular views of the Magellan Straits greet us on arrival, as does Hector, our waiter for the evening. Hector is shortish, with a moustache, in his early sixties and with a style very similar to Manuel of *Fawlty Towers* fame, complete with a frustrating 'Que?' Hector speaks Spanish only and shuffles his feet in a comedic manner. You can hear him before you can see him. We suggest that the window table is good for us. Hector gets a little upset, as the table isn't completely set, and points at another table in the middle of the restaurant with no view. Quickly surmising that the view may well be the highlight of our dining experience, we insist on sitting at our table of choice. Hector caves in and reluctantly finishes setting our table by bringing over one knife and one napkin.

Restaurante Panorámico / Panoramic Restaurante

Style & Quality

The other staff begin to arrive for the evening shift. All are impeccably labelled. The first is a young lady, Sophia, who sits quietly at the cashier's seat filing her nails and sending text messages; there is absolutely no way in the world that she will get out of her seat until the shift is over. A young man, Juan, seems to be in charge of the bar – not actually serving drinks, just in charge of the general area. The next to arrive is Max, a very upright and professional-looking man. There is hope for us yet, we think. Another is a middle-aged woman, Zina, who arrives and starts chatting to Sophia. There are now five staff to serve, well, only us. The tables are not set, the bar is not prepared and the staff are all having a lovely time chatting when, without warning, twenty customers arrive at the door. Hector, who seems to specialise in tasks that do not generate revenue, seats them expertly before pouring each a glass of water. There are now five tables of patrons in the restaurant. Menus are given to some but not all the tables; a menu shortage is suspected. Anticipating the looming logjam of orders, we try in vain to get some attention. After a few minutes we are successful as Max approaches our table. We place our orders with Max. 'Bread?' enquires Max. 'Thank you,' we chorus.

The task of getting the bread is quickly taken over by Hector, who shakes a bag filled with dinner rolls out onto a baking dish before placing them under the grill for a quick warm-up. How thoughtful. But Hector has become distracted by several empty water glasses, which he rushes about filling. The owners of these glasses are eager to order a meal, but Hector has no interest in these requests and ignores the patrons completely. Sophia is still chatting with Zina; Max is passing menus from one table to the next, presumably taking meal orders, and Juan is overwhelmed at the bar, with five orders in front of him and no bottle opener.

At this point I lean forward to check what is happening in the kitchen, with particular reference to the grill, and glance over just in time to see the flame leap across the bread rolls and out of the griller. The restaurant is filling with smoke. The ladies chatting at the cashier are oblivious, but Hector is onto it. Almost breaking out of his shuffle, he slinks into the kitchen and flings the tray out from under the griller sending 30 flaming rolls flying across the kitchen like shooting stars, scalding his fingers in the process. At this point, three more tables arrive and are seated by Max. We now have a full house, and the patrons are growing restless as Hector furiously crawls about on the kitchen floor gathering the rolls and scraping the burnt bits off each roll with a fork!

Juan returns from wherever it was he had to go to find a bottle opener; Zina drags herself away from her conversation with Sophia to distribute the drinks Juan has now managed to put up on the bar, and Max is still taking orders. Now all the patrons have drinks and have ordered their meals. Hector shuffles about the restaurant with a tray of partially incinerated rolls, which are quickly snapped up by the hungry patrons. Almost an hour has passed since we sat down, and it has been 40 minutes for everyone else. Several tables are becoming restless; two try to establish the whereabouts of their meals with no success. One table walks out, then another. These walkouts go unnoticed by all staff members. At this point the owner arrives – we know he is the owner because he is the only person without a name tag. A tall, handsome man in his fifties, he sashays towards the cashier. 'This will be good,' we mutter to ourselves, hoping for a dressing down of the ineffectual staff. What will he do to pull them into line? He casually positions himself at the cashier station and proceeds to make phone call after phone call, only pausing to order a coffee. The lunatics have taken over the asylum.

We have been seated for an hour and a half; the entertainment has been so brilliant that it is almost a disappointment when our meals finally arrive. Two more tables walk out. The restaurant is now only two-thirds full, and we are the first to see any food. Hector looks around and seems almost relieved. He tops up some unattended water glasses and reshuffles napkins and cutlery on the newly vacated tables. The fifth and sixth tables are about to leave without eating when the meal trolley emerges from the lift, laden with salads, which are distributed to all tables. Except for the lettuce, all the salad ingredients have come from a can, only adding to the intrigue: how could it take over an hour to make twenty salads? Perhaps the bottle opener that Juan found was needed in the kitchen to open the cans. Who knows? We leave a large tip for encouragement and entertainment value. Perhaps they should advertise as a theatre restaurant.

WEATHER UPDATE ✳✳✳

Wind never dipped below 15 knots. Runway re-drifting. Wind 21 knots gusting 34 knots. Wind 21 knots gusting 33 knots. Wind 20 knots gusting 44 knots. Wind 17 knots gusting 31 knots. Keeping it short – too tired. Runway clear but re-drifting. Wind 9 knots gusting 29 knots. Wind 11 knots gusting 32 knots. There are large masses of cloud. More encouraging today than previous few days. No fly day. ✳✳✳

And so it continues. This is our life for six days in Punta, receiving these boring, seemingly hopeless weather forecasts. We cannot stray far from town as conditions are likely to change very quickly, and the window of opportunity only opens briefly in Antarctica. It is hardly surprising that we eventually turn to drink.

To add insult to injury, the Hotel Finis Terrae kicks us out since we have only booked for three nights, and we are forced to move to the somewhat less salubrious Hostal de la Avenida. Keen to let off some steam, we go out drinking, settling in for the night at a cosy bar. The Boss is in fine form, telling stories of his time in Antarctica, and Mertz is very entertaining, amusing us with his dry observations. The sense of anticipation could not be any more intense. The British crew bound for the South Pole arrive for a few beers then leave us to dine at the only Chinese restaurant in town before returning for more beers.

We must have been sitting in this bar for over five hours by now and I am feeling more than a little cheeky. Given that Australians always like to give the English a good-natured ribbing about whatever we can get away with, I take it upon myself to give them heaps about their planned drive to the South Pole in the converted Ford – the *Global Challenger*. To Jason, the leader: 'You know that this drive of yours will either be an overwhelming success or total disaster, don't you? The chances of you falling into a crevasse have to be high. How will you get out? Not that I am wishing you ill, but it would be interesting if you did in fact drive into a rather large crevasse. Now that would be a challenge for the *Global Challenger*.'

Just to ensure that enough was being done to strain Australian–English relations, I then decide to dish out a friendly slap to the cheek of a delightful chap, Andrew, with whom I have been chatting for the past hour. The mood quickly changes as the slap registers on the faces of those around us. One wants to defend me (thank you, Mertz); one wants to punch my lights out (totally understandable, Richard), and the rest just want to leave, which they do, leaving the boozing buffoons Mertz, the Boss and myself, Oates, at the bar. We decide it is time to go. The Boss asks, 'What the hell happened back there? I didn't see a thing.' Mertz interjects, 'Old Oates just slapped one of our friends across the face with an open hand and they all left. Didn't you hear it, Boss? The whole bar heard it before they saw it.' 'Jeepers Oates,' says the Boss. 'Looks like we won't be getting a lift in that Ford.' The Boss, Mertz and Oates burst into hysterical laughter as they wander down the streets of Punta.

That night on the way home, we observe an unusual phenomenon, which none of us has ever seen before or since. We look south down Avenue Chiloé and see a bright glow from the sun in the sky. But looking north up Avenue Chiloé, the sky is pitch black. Normally, if part of the sky is illuminated, the rest of the sky at least has a glow, but on this occasion the sky was completely black. We are fortunate to observe this oddity of nature, which only occurs this far south.

WEATHER UPDATE ❋❋❋

Patriot Hills is centre of static cloudbank. Another enemy now is lack of winds, making runway clearing a slow process. Hope the wind picks up for a few hours today then drops to current levels. Cloud base lifted but still unpleasant conditions. The winds started to drop. The winds stopped. The clouds have moved over. The clouds now sit. Wind 25 knots gusting 28 knots. Wind 32 knots gusting 36 knots. Hoping for blue skies tomorrow. No fly day. ❋❋❋

The Boss and Mertz outside the Hostal de la Avenida

My first job the next day is to find the British expedition and to apologise to Andrew in particular and the team in general for my rudeness. The cheap talk was OK, but the slap was totally uncalled for. My behaviour was completely uncharacteristic, and I have shocked even myself. Thankfully we find the Brits by lunchtime and apologise. They are fine about it, and we chat with them all for a while before returning to bed. Mertz arrives back at the room to find a bill for US$80, which is what the hotel charges for a damp mattress. Nice one, Mertz! We ponder together the consequences if we have to depart today. We make a declaration: no more drinking until we return to Punta!

Thankfully the weather is still poor and there is no chance of a flight today. The Boss and I go for a long walk with our cameras along the foreshore, where a long, rickety line of timber houses enjoy absolute waterfront views. These dwellings are precariously perched

Beach combing at Punta Arenas

on a hillside facing the Magellan Straits. They are made of tin and timber, and if it were not for the occasional dog and washing hanging on a line, you would swear that they were deserted a long time ago, such is their state of disrepair. Seeing this kind of poverty makes us realise again how lucky we are to live the lives we do. Food, clothing and shelter are taken for granted at home, but here they are precious commodities.

We cannot believe the amount of rubbish. There is junk everywhere, and the toilets flush directly onto the beach; the Boss notes that it resembles a tip. At that moment, a tip truck backs up and dumps a load of rubble and rubbish at our feet. This is an odd place. Surely you would protect the town beach from this sort of activity. Apparently not. What would I know? You can only assume that the government is preoccupied with more important issues than public health and sanitation.

Absolute beach front properties in Punta Arenas

PROHIBIDO EL ACCESO
PELIGRO
RELIQUIA HISTORICA

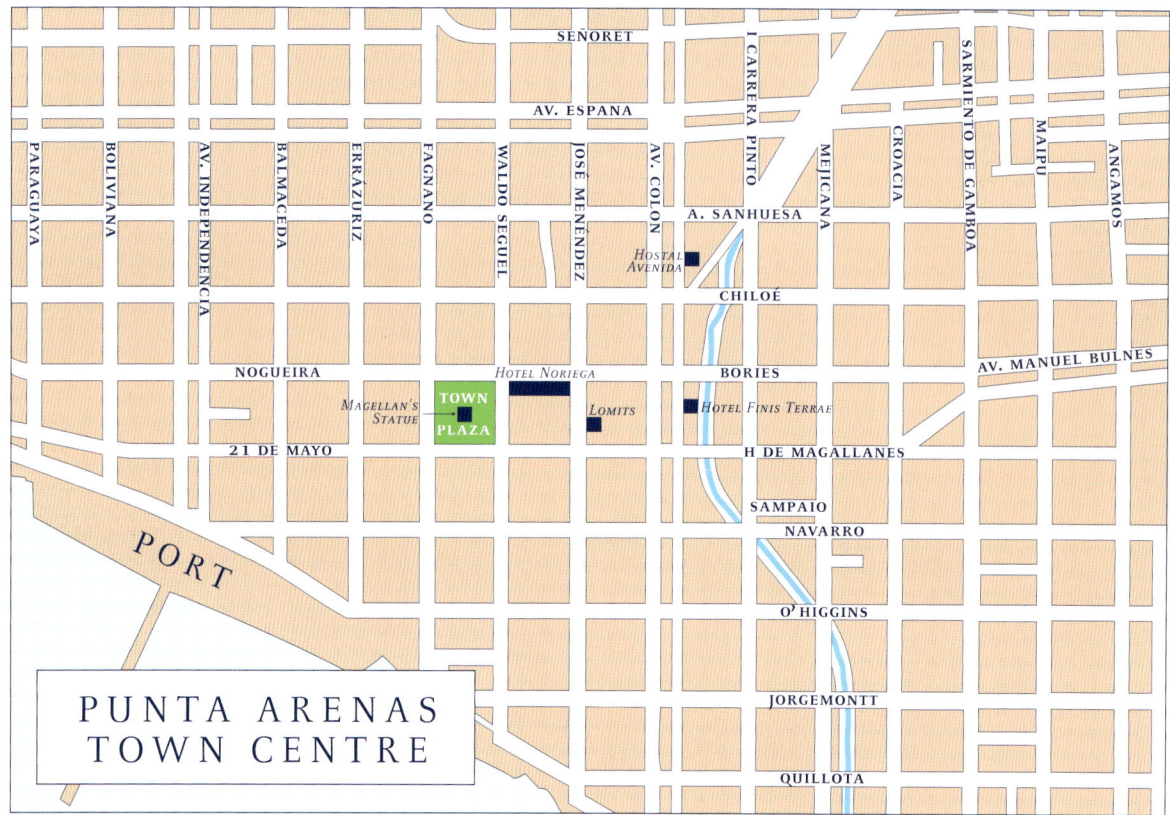

PUNTA ARENAS
TOWN CENTRE

Two more days pass in Punta without incident. Mertz celebrates his 39th birthday. I give him an insulated balaclava (face mask) for the trek south as the one that he has brought along is alarmingly lightweight and totally inadequate for what lies ahead. We take Mertz out to the Hotel Noriega for some lamb cutlets and a birthday cake and candles. The entire restaurant joins in when we sing Mertz 'Happy Birthday'.

We spend a morning in the huge walled Cementerio Municipal. There is something deeply moving and fascinating about the cemeteries of Latin America and this one includes sculpture gardens, a huge sarcophagus, extravagant tombs, elaborate monuments, very well-attended grave sites and something that I have not seen before – the 'cemetery as motel'. There are rows and rows of a structure resembling a low-rise motel. Coffins are housed here in individual slots, and the small openings are sealed over and covered with small plaques and decorated with flowers or porcelain photographs. It is very peaceful.

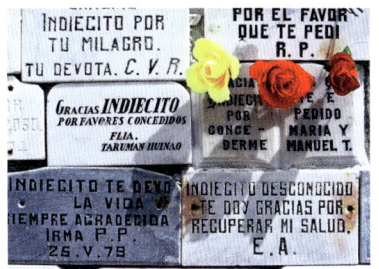

The Cementerio Municipal in Punta Arenas

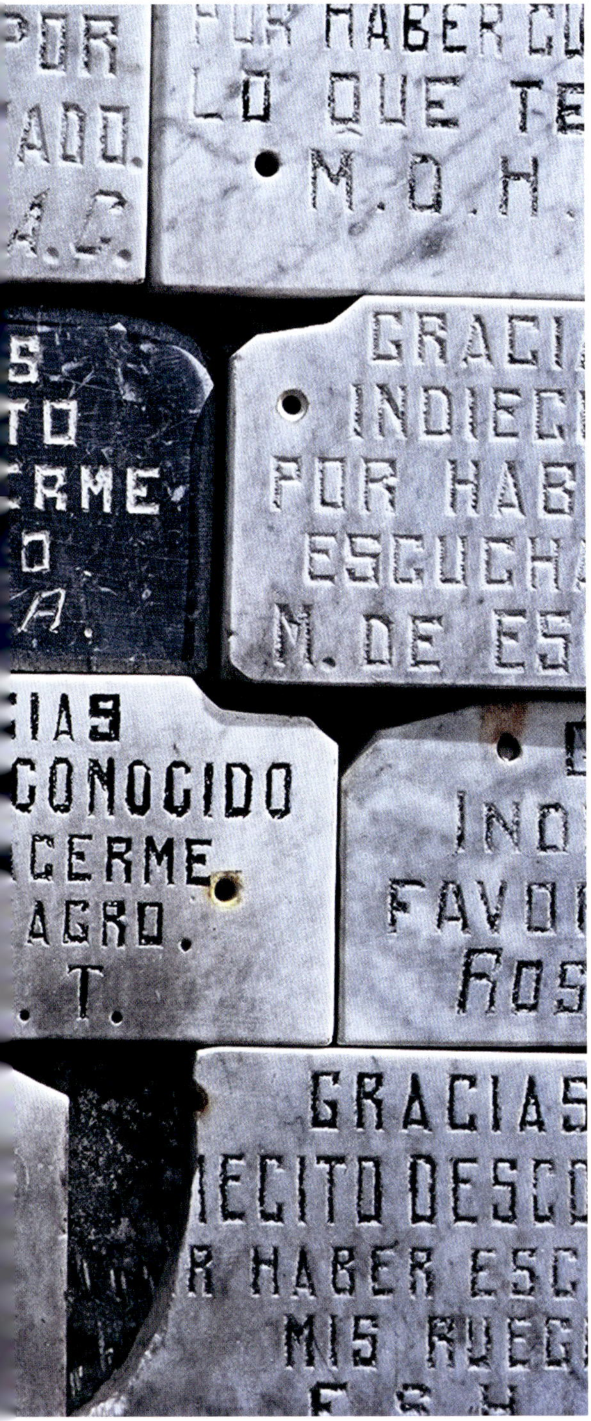
LO QUE TE
M.O.H.
GRACI
INDIEC
POR HAB
ESCUCH
M. DE ES
CONOCIDO
CERME
AGRD.
FAVO
GRACIAS
IECITO DESC
R HABER ESC
MIS RUEG

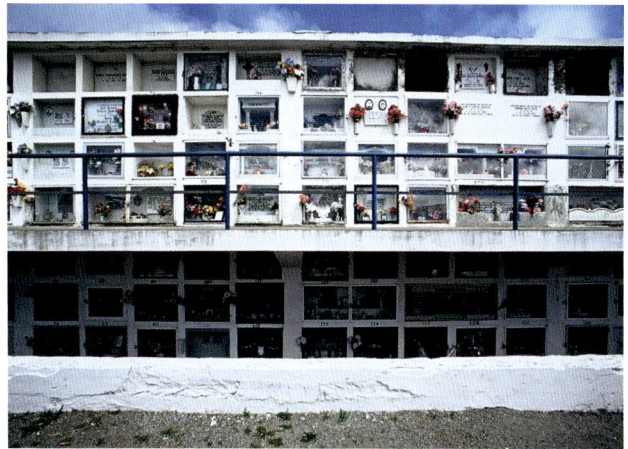

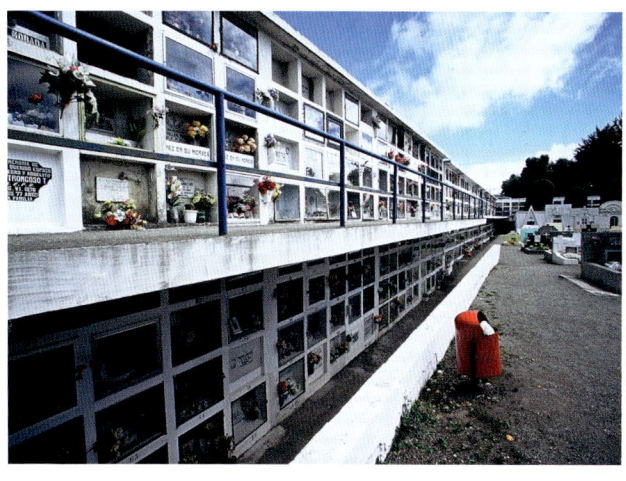

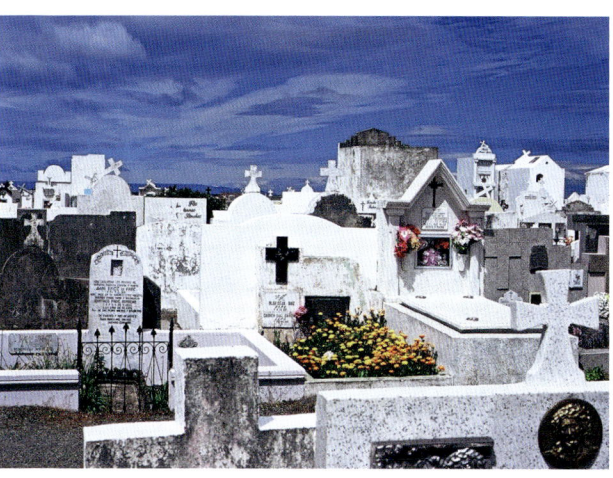

María Bernarda Barría Cárcamo
✱20 · 10 · 1921
† 17 · 12 · 2004
Nanita: Recuerdo de sus hijos, yerno, nuera y nietos.

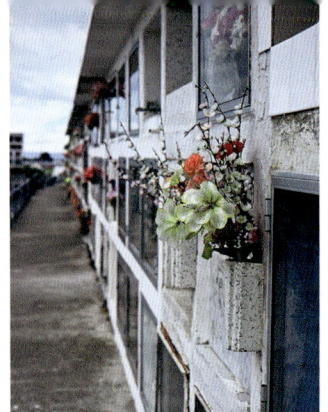

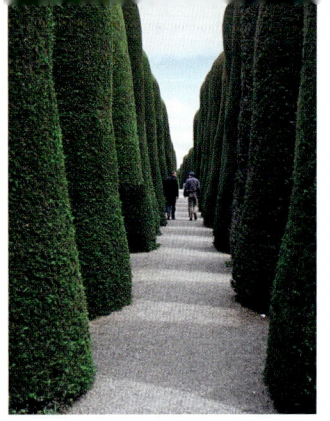

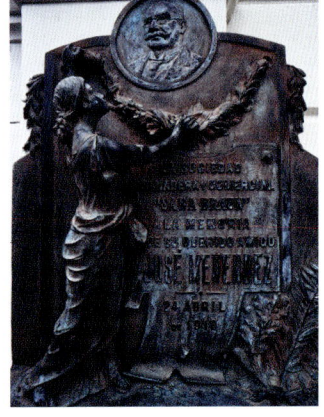

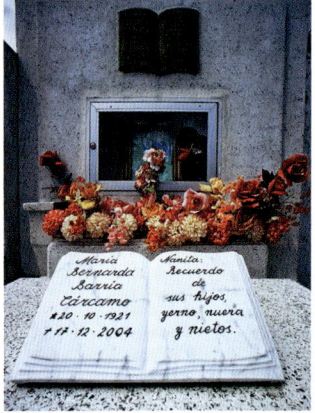

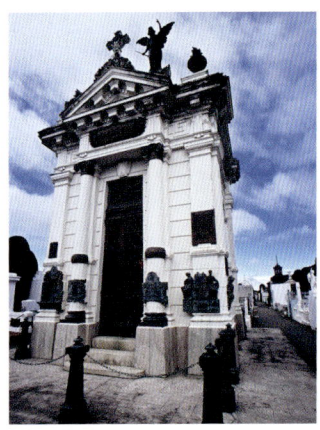

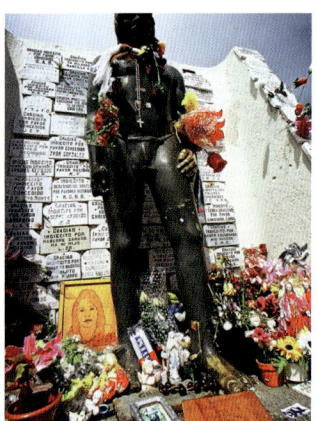

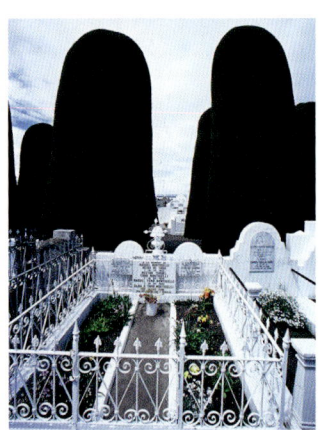

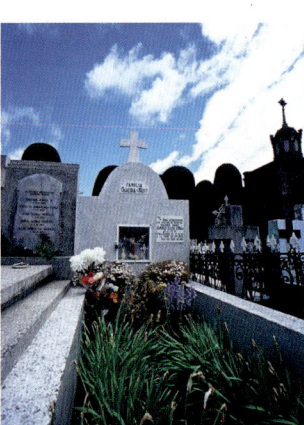

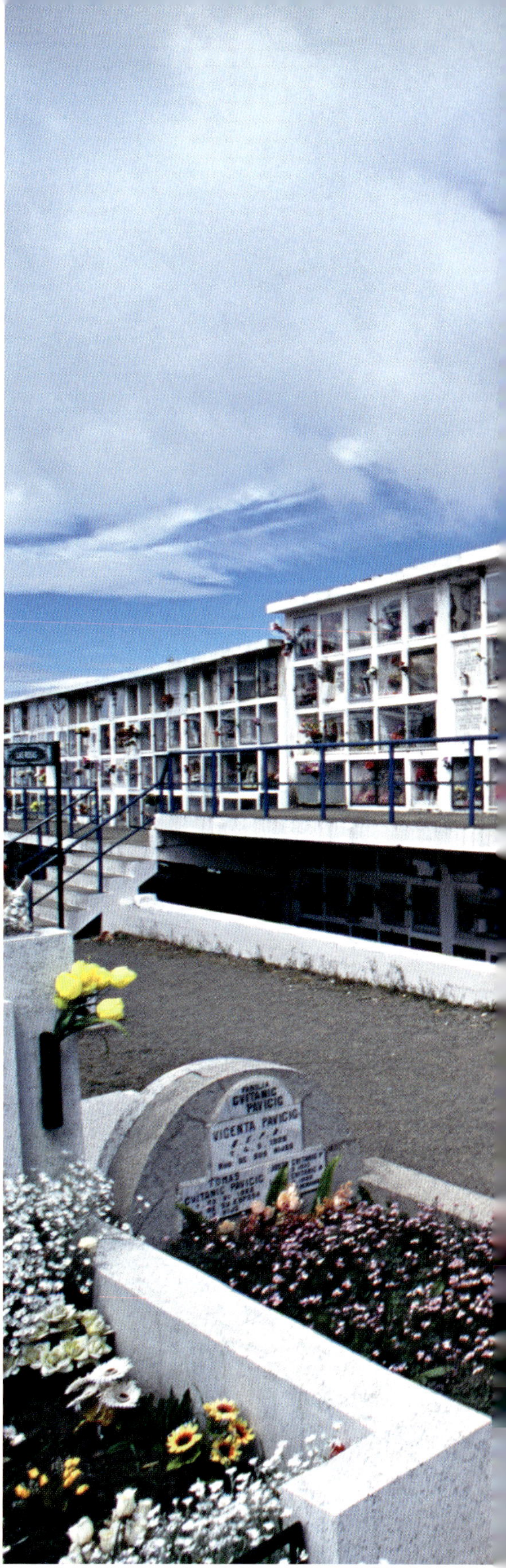
FAMILIA
CVITANIC
PAVICIC
VICENTA PAVICIC

WEATHER UPDATE ❄❄❄

Winds jumpy all night. Wind behaving well in last hour. Winds took downward dip in last hour. Wind direction has steadied this morning, but shortly after noon the wind has picked up to much higher levels again. Wind 22 knots gusting 30 knots. Wind 23 knots gusting 37 knots. Wind 11 knots gusting 23 knots. Wind 14 knots gusting 19 knots. Some gusts exceeded 40 knots in that time. A bit less gloom and doom than yesterday. Let's hope for a miracle. Heavy spindrift coming off hills. Blowing snow has reduced visibility. A hole overhead letting in a little sun but poor ground visibility. Looking better. ❄❄❄

We get a call the next morning suggesting that the wind is settling and that if this pattern continues to hold there is a chance for a flight some time today. They will call us again at 2 p.m.

As we wander the streets, the Boss runs into an old friend, Geoff Somers, who has just arrived in town and is preparing to follow in the footsteps of Scott's expedition using exactly the same gear as Scott used in 1911–12. It is remarkable listening to this man and hearing about some of his experiences, which include the first totally unsupported traverse of Greenland by dogsled from the south to the north at its longest point (in 1989). This feat was a mere training run for Geoff's adventures the following year, when he was a member of the first and longest traverse of the Antarctic continent by dogsled and ski – a distance of some 6400 kilometres. The team began at the tip of the Antarctic Peninsula, went via the South Pole and reached the Antarctic east coast at Mirny 220 days later. Geoff has also completed several successful treks to the South and North Poles, as well as crossing the Great Sandy Desert and the Gibson Desert in Australia by camel.

Here we are chatting to him in the street about how he recreated some of the gear that was used by Scott. We are dumbstruck as he tells us how he tracked down the exact type of rattan used in Scott's equipment, which grows in a rainforest in South-East Asia but is no longer harvested. He sourced the plant and had some cut down and sent to him in order to manufacture ski poles identical to those used by Scott and his men in 1911. The level of expertise, dedication and commitment displayed by Geoff is just unbelievable. He has been awarded the Polar Medal and the MBE. Oh, the people you meet!

We are now into the first week of December. Just as we are beginning to wonder whether we will ever get to Antarctica, we receive good news. There is further steady improvement in the weather at Patriot Hills. The call comes through at 2 p.m. and we are put on high alert, whatever that means. It certainly sounds very dramatic. It is also suddenly sounding very likely that our flight will depart tonight. We receive the next call at 5 p.m. and are instructed to get ourselves ready for collection in 45 minutes. We are off to the airport! We pack, the bus collects us, and we are on our way.

On arrival at the airport we must pass through customs, even though we are travelling to the Chilean claim in Antarctica – any excuse for a stamp from an official. Mertz, the Boss and I are the last three to be processed by the lone customs official, who takes one look at our passports and becomes instantly animated. He begins raving in Spanish, raising his voice and waving our passports above his head. This is not good! Mark, our logistics operator in Punta, is called over to make sense of the situation. After a long and heated conversation in Spanish, it is established that the over-zealous customs official from last week has inadvertently stamped us *out* of Chile. So now, according to our passports, we have illegally entered the country and should be arrested. This is surely the last thing we need. Mark talks some sense into the customs official, who eventually calms down and rolls back the dates on his stamp and stamps us back in, then out again. The ink is flying; the dates are rolling; the customs official is absolutely loving all this stamping. Beware the man bearing a stamp in South America!

We walk up the ramp at the back end of the Ilyushin jet and find our seats. There are only two tiny windows on each side; the seats face each other, with all the cargo, including a 5-ton Ford truck, in the middle. The Ilyushin is an extraordinary aircraft, possibly the most practical machine I have ever experienced. It has a high wing, four jets and 20 wheels, with a payload of 48 000 kilograms. The bulk of the payload is fuel. Every activity in Antarctica is fuel dependant. Fuel is super expensive in Antarctica: US$2000 per barrel (44-gallon drum) at Patriot Hills, and US$25 000 per barrel at the South Pole. Sitting on the hard bench seat and buckling up, I feel as if I am in a World War II movie, preparing to parachute behind enemy lines.

Three of the Russian crew are in position up the front, leaving the fourth to run through the safety procedures. The engines have started, and the safety officer has to shout to be heard above the din as he briefs us in a very heavy Russian accent: 'You vill do za belt tight, da! Vhen ve lose za air ... *nyet, nyet* ... If, *if* ve lose za air ... Sohry, sohry! You vill take zis mask ant poll it on za face, *da!'* That is it; the safety brief is finished. This is flying Russian-style.

At this point I reach under my seat to check that I have said mask. Fumbling around, I find the mask and tug at it to inspect it. The bloody thing comes off in my hand. I have just disconnected my lifeline. The jet lurches forward. It is too late to unbuckle myself and get under the seat to reconnect the rubber tube, so I continue to fumble about with the nozzle, causing a cramp to shoot down my shoulder. I fiddle about until I finally succeed in reconnecting the rubber air tube to the oxygen supply nozzle.

The noise is now incredible as the engines power up and are readied for take-off. Nothing, however, can prepare us for what we are about to experience. Looking straight ahead across a mountain of barrels strapped down with a cargo net, I detect a strong smell of fuel hanging heavy in the air. What's that? Surely not! Yes, I can also smell smoke. Quickly glancing around the aircraft, I notice that all the other passengers are looking madly about for the source of the smoke. What bloody idiot could possibly be smoking in such an environment?

Interior of the Russian Ilyushin jet

A few passengers shout out for the smoker to come clean and put the damned thing out before it is put out for them. But no one owns up. Then we hear a voice from the front of the aircraft, shouting above the roar of the engine, 'It's all right. It's only the pilot.' Only the pilot! Does this mean that he knows what he is doing, or is he just an absolute moron? We hope desperately for the former.

Further on, past the fuel barrels, I can see the tops of the heads of the other passengers facing us. The small, dull ceiling lights are glowing softly, and nothing can be seen through the two windows on either side of the aircraft from any seated position. The noise grows even louder as the pilot makes his final checks before letting the Ilyushin go. When he does let it go, I feel like it is about to explode. Everything vibrates and shakes, I am convinced that I have read in an article somewhere that a jet will vibrate violently just before it explodes. I am a poor flyer at the best of times, but this is simply outrageous. If I could get off now, I would. I am glad that I can't, but I would if I could. The aircraft is now hurtling down the runway, and the g force pulling on me – and I am sitting sideways, don't forget – feels four or five times stronger than that of any commercial jet experience. I feel like an astronaut for a few minutes, such is the sensation of power and speed. (This may or may not be scientifically correct, but that is how I feel.) The experience of lift-off is strangely different without a window, and it is disconcerting for a nervous flyer not to be able to look outside to get a sense of how everything is going. My only comfort is the roar of the engines: I want them to stay nice and loud.

Now that the worst is over and the Ilyushin has levelled out, I calm down somewhat. The Boss and I head for the window to check what we are passing over. I stay at or near the window for the entire journey, backing away only temporarily when another passenger wants to have a look. The Boss has a wealth of knowledge of the area, having travelled down the Antarctic Peninsula by boat ten times. I take notes.

The flight time to Patriot Hills is estimated at four and a half hours. We pass over Tierra del Fuego, the 'land of fire', then over the Drake Passage, regarded as the most hostile on the planet, with huge swells, gale force winds and hazardous storms. We are now at 60 degrees south, the outer limit of the winter sea ice. This part of the ocean is known as the Antarctic Convergence, and this rich natural environment is a breeding ground for the basis of all life in Antarctica – plankton and krill. These tiny organisms form the base of the food chain.

As we pass over 66 degrees south, we enter the Antarctic Circle and the region covered by the Antarctic Treaty. Within this imaginary line, the sun never sets during the height of summer and never rises through the depths of winter. The weather is clear, and the first icebergs come into view, bright beacons of white against the dark ocean. Their wave smashed tips protrude slightly from the ocean with their massive bulk sitting beneath the water, disappearing slowly into the inky blue depths below. As we pass over the Bellingshausen Sea to the west of the Antarctic Peninsula, we see the great mass of sheet ice pushing against itself and rising up in ridges where the pressure becomes too great. At this point I am invited to sit up front with the navigator, who sits below the pilots in the split-level flight deck. The views from this vantage point are breathtaking, if a little frightening. The navigator has a transparent floor made of thick panels of a clear plastic compound, which affords a 180-degree view ahead and below. I can see the Ellsworth Mountains looming ahead of us, and as we approach them, the southern end of the blue ice airstrip comes into view. It's mostly kept clear of snow by the terrific force of the katabatic winds that thunder down the mountains. While these winds are fabulous for keeping snow off the airstrip, they are dreadful when you need still conditions in which to land, as we have learnt during our inglorious six days in Punta. It is time to sit down, strap in and hold on.

Landing is interesting: we surge up and over and down again, across the natural rolls in the ice. It is like being on a boat and rolling with the swell. Finally the Ilyushin rolls to a halt. We have arrived in Antarctica.

Chapter 5

HORSESHOE VALLEY, ANTARCTICA

After nine months of planning, training, gear-gathering, list-checking and travelling, we are here. The weather is perfect: not a breath of wind; clear blue skies; brilliant sunshine; a temperature of −15°C. The time is 3.40 a.m. I shuffle down the stairs at the back of the Ilyushin onto the very, very slick blue ice. These are my first steps on the frozen continent, so I move with enormous care and trepidation as I have heard many horror stories of broken arms and dislocated shoulders through lack of respect for this slick blue ice. Shuffling carefully, I reach the relative safety of the firm snow and grab Mertz and the Boss for a photo opportunity before beginning the 2-kilometre walk to Patriot Hills camp.

The camp is set up by ALE in early November and packed up at the end of January, operating for only a short three-month season. We are invited into the mess tent for a meal. Waiting in the tent are a group of four climbers just back from Mount Vinson (the highest peak on the continent) who are returning to Punta Arenas. The weather on Mount Vinson has been dreadful, and it shows clearly in the men's faces. Wally Berg, a good friend of the Boss, guided this group. Given their condition we can only imagine what these men have just endured. It is considered bad form to question a recently returned group about their success or otherwise.

ANTARCTICA

SOUTH ATLANTIC OCEAN

SOUTH GEORGIA

FALKLAND ISLANDS

Novolazarevskaya, Russia

NEUMAYER, GERMANY

MAITRI, INDIA

Syowa, Japan

Weddell Sea

SANAE IV, SOUTH AFRICA

General Bernardo O'Higgins, Chile

Esperanza, Argentina

Academician Vernadsky, Ukraine

HALLEY, UNITED KINGDOM

Punta Arenas

ROTHERA, UNITED KINGDOM

General-Belgrano II, Argentina

Mawson, Australia

SOUTH AMERICA

ANTARCTIC PENINSULA

Ronne Ice Shelf

80°

Zhongshan, China

ACADEMICIAN VERNADSKI, Ukraine

PROGRESS II, Russia

Patriot Hills

SOUTH POLE

Amundsen-Scott, USA

Mirny, Russia

Vostok, Russia

Ross Ice Shelf

Concordia, France & Italy

Casey, Australia

McMurdo, USA

Scott, New Zealand

SOUTHERN OCEAN

Dumont d'Urville, France

SCALE

0   1600 KILOMETRES

ICE SHELF   BASES

NEW ZEALAND   AUSTRALIA

Ilyushin fly over

Wally is a remarkable man. He has reached the summit of Mount Everest (8850 metres) four times; he has been to the top of Mount McKinley in Alaska (6194 metres) four times, Mount Elbrus in Russia (5633 metres) three times, the Carstensz Pyramid in New Guinea (4884 metres) twice, Mount Kilimanjaro in Tanzania (5895 metres) 25 times, Mount Aconcagua in Argentina (6962 metres) once and Mount Vinson in Antarctica (4897 metres) twice. Wally is the world's premier 'Seven Summits' mountaineer. A more delightful man you will not meet, and despite his recent ordeal he is nothing but kind, engaging and interesting. Oh, the people you meet.

Wally and his group have only arrived back in Patriot Hills that night on the Twin Otter aircraft that is used by ALE to ferry climbers to and from Mount Vinson. They too had been waiting for a break in the weather at Vinson so that they could be picked up by the Twin Otter. These men all have a look in their eyes, a certain expression that I have seen only once before. It was in the Andes in 1992 as I was preparing for my first mountaineering expedition with Peter Hillary. Our plan was to climb to the summit of Mount Aconcagua, the highest peak outside of the Himalayas. The day before departure, we entered the dining room at the Hotel del Inca to find four ragged climbers in filthy, shredded climbing gear, seemingly frozen still and not blinking, just staring straight ahead. The group had left as six and returned as four. Two of their party lay dead on the mountain. I named this look the 'Thousand Mile Stare'. This mountaineering is serious stuff. (For a full account of this 1992 climb, go to my website, www.sunburntcountry.net) It is 4.45 a.m. as we sit down to a meal in the mess tent with Wally Berg. Wally takes our photograph. He is very excited for us and about the trek we are to undertake. Wally and his men are called for the Ilyushin's departure.

As we bid them farewell, we cannot help but notice that Wally has a split down the middle of each thumb, beginning at the tip and running down the thumb pad to the first knuckle. Each split appears to be very deep, almost to the bone. They look incredibly painful. I ask the Boss what might have caused such a nasty wound. 'I think Wally had a pretty rough time up on Vinson by the look of him and his pals. The thumb will split when exposed to extremes of temperature.' On hearing this, I rub my thumbs vigorously inside my gloves.

We watch as the Ilyushin takes off with a roar before swinging around sharply to make a low pass over the Patriot Hills camp, which is greeted with great enthusiasm by all. We are weary now; it is 6 a.m. and the sun is still shining brilliantly. We erect the tents before collapsing into our bags at 7 a.m., exhausted.

The tents are very small and low to the ground, which is useful for sitting out a storm but terrible for pretty much anything else. You cannot even kneel in them without getting your head caught up in the drying line that criss-crosses the ceiling. The tent is your best friend and your worst enemy. You love it when it is erect and decked out waiting for you; you hate it when it is flailing about in your hands as you attempt to get the damned thing to serve its purpose. There is also one question that you never want to hear or ask: 'Where's the bloody tent?'

We wake, pack up the tents, get a briefing from the camp manager, pack our sledges and are away. Feelings of liberation, isolation, joy and foreboding overwhelm me as the Patriot Hills camp disappears behind us.

We are on our skis, carrying our backpacks and man-hauling our sledges in this magnificent frozen valley. The only forms of life we will see for the next two weeks are each other. The Horseshoe Valley is a very impressive landscape – silent and clean – and it reminds me of another favourite wide-open space that is silent and clean: the Australian desert.

In adventure circles, the area through which we are travelling is known as 'Deep Field'. I love this impressive moniker, it has a certain ring to it. During a leisurely five-hour haul we cover 20 kilometres before setting up camp. The day is glorious: brilliant sunshine, still air, clear skies and a mild −15°c. We have only been in Antarctica for eighteen hours but we have been very busy: tents have been erected twice and collapsed once; all our gear has been packed onto sledges for the trek; the snow wall around the tent has been built twice; all bags, sleeping gear and our general kit have been unpacked, packed and unpacked again. We cook up a katabatic hoosh for dinner before falling into a deeply restorative twelve-hour sleep.

Hoosh time

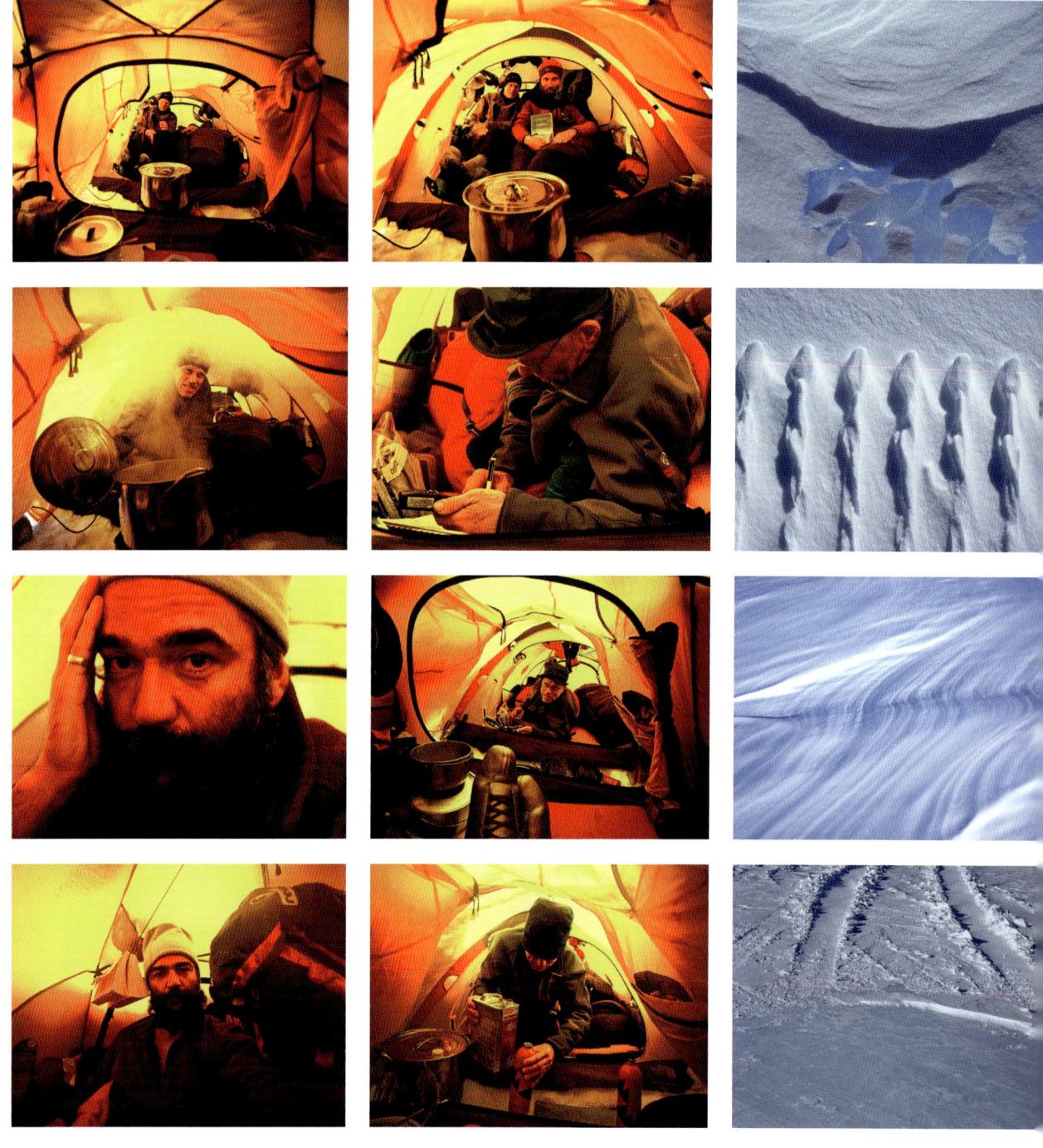

It is unusual for me to sleep this long or this well in a tent. The tent is relatively comfortable, but let's be clear: it is not a bedroom. We sleep on wafer-thin inflatable mattresses, which in turn sit atop thin, lightweight Styrofoam roll-up mats. The tent floor is less than a quarter of a millimetre thick and provides little or no insulation. The best place to pitch the tent is on firm, packed snow. The ground is never flat, so we must landscape the surface as best we can in order to get something close to a flat surface on which to sleep. This we do with stomping boots, shovel and ice axe. Once satisfied that the surface is as flat as we can get it, all the cooking gear, sleeping gear and food for the night are passed into the tent. The trouble starts here. If you are not careful, it is easy to put a knee dent in the freshly levelled snow right in the middle of where your bed will go. This knee dent will quickly freeze solid, making it impossible to remove without moving the tent and ensuring a shockingly uncomfortable night's sleep. So when erecting the tent I move carefully and spread my weight evenly lest I ruin my level bed space. There is a lot to think about.

But even before I can contemplate getting into the tent, the snow wall needs to be built. This is constructed around the entire southern side of the tent from west to east, facing into the katabatic winds. The purpose of the snow wall is to ease the wind pressure on the tent, making it less likely to be shredded by the katabatic, which has been known to blow relentlessly for weeks on end. The snow saw is the implement of choice for this job.

Ideally you try to cut the compacted snow into rectangular blocks and stack them as you would a Lego wall. If the snow is densely packed but not solid ice, the task is relatively straightforward and can be completed in an hour or so. An assembly-line grid pattern is established by the cutter for sawing the blocks from the compacted snow. Once cut out, the blocks need to be popped out with the shovel.

Mertz is very good with the snow saw and lifting heavy things, so he naturally drifts to the role of cutter and popper, leaving me to carry and stack the blocks. The wall will typically be 1–1.5 metres high so that it at least covers the height of the tent. Some of our creations just get the job done; some are works of art. All are practical and physically exhausting. That is the thing about life at 80 degrees south: everything takes time and effort. When you consider all that you do in a day and the conditions in which you do them, a day in the Antarctic is the equivalent of spending the entire day in the gym – no wonder we are exhausted.

The snow wall is built and the tents erected. The Boss and Mertz will stay outside and ensure that all the guy ropes are secure and all the points of the tent are fixed with ice axes and snow anchors (a stuff sack attached to a guy rope, filled with snow and buried). I can slip into the tent now – watch the knee dents!

I have organised all the freeze-dried meals, and bought and packaged all the food, so it stands to reason that I am the cook. I love cooking and wouldn't have it any other way. Cooking is a wonderful opportunity to care for and nurture the group. People who don't enjoy cooking often fail to appreciate the joy of being able to prepare meals for loved ones. I have now carefully laid out my bed and assumed my position by the stove – the lifeblood of the trek – without which we die. Mertz has banned himself from any direct contact with the stove in light of his legendary heavy-handedness.

The stove lives in its own stuff bag. It is connected to a fuel bottle, which is given a quick pump to pressurise the liquid before lighting. Great caution is needed here. You are lighting a stove in a highly flammable tent that is hanging less than a metre above and around the burning flame. I let a little liquid from the bottle onto the jet. If the pressure is too great, a gush of liquid will fill the jet, making it unsafe to light. If I get it just right, enough fuel will fill the jet and it will be ready to light. I light the jet, which always ignites with a big magician's 'poof!' I now hover over the stove with a pot lid, deflecting any leaping flames from the tent walls and ceiling, and wait for the flame to settle down and heat the coil before letting any more fuel out of the bottle. Lighting the stove is, without doubt, the high-wire act of any expedition. If the tent goes, so do we. The flame settles and I open up the fuel a fraction. The coil is now hot, vaporising the fuel as it passes through, and the stove is firing – a particularly comforting sound.

My next job is to start melting snow for hot drinks and dinner. The Boss and Mertz are still outside fixing all the guy ropes and generally ensuring that the tent is bomb-proof. Mertz has made a pile of manageable snow blocks outside the meeting point of the two tents, which can be easily accessed from inside for the snow pot. I empty the thermos flasks of hot water into the snow pot and begin to add snow. A trap for young players here is to place too much snow and too little water in the pot as the snow absorbs the water and the bottom can burn out of the pot – very bad form. Haven't done it; don't want to do it. A thermos is the only receptacle that will keep the water from refreezing. You don't carry a water bottle in Antarctica; you carry a thermos. The stove is roaring, the snow melting. The next task is to make a hot drink for the Boss, Mertz and myself. As soon as there is enough boiling water, I fill up two thermos flasks and secure the lids. Now more snow goes into the pot, and the lid goes on.

Mertz is coming into the tent now and passing me his boots and pack. I am alone in this tent (referred to as '1A' by Mertz, in an allusion to a first-class seat), but to balance this relative luxury, I must store all the food, packs and boots. Mertz calls out for the Boss to come in. The Boss passes his boots and pack through into what has begun to resemble an old-fashioned Chinese laundry. I have swapped my day socks for bed socks and booties. The day socks hang from the tangle of clothesline across the tent ceiling. I take drinks orders from the men. The offering in the first week is extensive: five varieties of instant soup, eight flavours of electrolyte, coffee, four kinds of tea, hot chocolate and milk. What a spread!

As I finish making and pouring the hot drinks, my attention shifts to dinner. Our dehydrated meals have been ordered from and lovingly prepared by Nathan at Chefsway in Moonah, Tasmania, who specialises in making expedition meals for trips such as ours. We ordered the meals some months ago and are delighted with the quality. Nathan has made over 2500 meals for expeditions to Antarctica. The dinner options are perused: mushroom risotto, spaghetti Bolognese, beef curry and pasta primavera. Hmm! Curry it is. I empty the contents of the pre-packaged meal into the cooking pot and fill it with water to the line that I measured and marked on the pot some weeks ago. Oil and herbs are added to the hoosh. This meal will now be left to self-hydrate for half an hour while we concentrate on other tasks.

Mertz and the Boss are keen for a second round of drinks. I take their orders as they recline in their bags. I am hunched over the stove – as any good cook would be – making hot drinks and sending them out. More snow is now required to fill the pot, so I remove the lid. This instantly fills the tents with steam. I scoop up more snow.

I pause for a minute to reflect and enjoy my own hot drink, reclining in my back-supporting camp seat. What a brilliant item this is – very simple and very practical. Another round of hot drinks, then I add some more water to the curry, fill up the thermos flasks and scoop more snow into the pot. Finally I put the curry on the stove for fifteen minutes before serving it with a lump of frozen cheese. This routine of melting, boiling, pouring, cooking, melting, boiling, pouring and cooking takes about three hours from the time I enter the tent. Being cook is a bloody busy yet very rewarding job.

Chapter 6

THE EPIC

The weather is so good at camp one that we decide to spend two nights here. We spend the day walking around and photographing nearby. As the air is so still, I ask Mertz if he will do some nude modelling in the frozen icefields (current temperature −15°c). To my delight and surprise, Mertz agrees straightaway, with only one question and one request: 'Where do you want me to stand?' and 'Please do not highlight any of the shrinkage that will inevitably occur.' What a guy!

It's a very amusing experience, with Mertz dashing about naked, setting up a shot and striking a pose before diving into his down suit to warm up. To the best of my knowledge, this is the first ever naked photographic shoot in Antarctica. This is the day for photography, and I make the most of it before returning to the tent to sleep and prepare for tomorrow. The Boss spends the day successfully repairing our number one stove which had become blocked sending a scare through the camp. Do you ever wish that you could squeeze a few extra hours into the day? Well, during the Antarctic summer you can, as many hours as you like – the sun never sets. This is perfect for finishing off a job, going for a walk or taking a photograph. Or for delivering that favourite gag when a tent mate asks you, late at night, 'Are you still reading?' You respond, 'Why? Is the light bothering you?'

The next day it is considerably cooler; clouds have moved in and the tent is buffeted by the gusting winds. We are all feeling energized after a relaxed day yesterday spent tinkering with gear, taking photographs and exploring. There is much discussion in the tents this morning about getting to the base of Minaret Peak, an impressive mountain tucked in behind the Marble Hills. We calculate that Minaret Peak is some 25 kilometres away and that the last 5 kilometres are mostly uphill and facing south into the katabatic winds, if they should get up. Camp one is packed up with a minimum of fuss.

We are becoming efficient at camping on the packed snow and ice. I pack my snacks for the day in the top of my backpack along with lunch for the team, and then, just as we are leaving, I take off my down jacket and put it in the very top of the backpack for easy access.

'Work cool, rest warm,' is the Antarctic traveller's motto. We pull out of camp one together, travelling three across. The first hour of the day is filled with light banter until the wind picks up and the Boss surges to the front. The Boss is a very efficient mover on the skis. He never looks like slowing or speeding ahead, maintaining a consistent, solid pace all day.

Later that morning, I slowly edge to the front of the group, moving through the massive Horseshoe Valley. As I travel along the valley floor, my mind drifts. I have had numerous discussions with the Boss about his book *In the Ghost Country: A Lifetime Spent on the Edge*. It is largely based on the Boss's brutal 72-day trek to the South Pole in 1998–99 with Eric Phillips and Jon Muir. During this ordeal, the Boss became estranged from his travelling companions and began to hallucinate while hauling his sledge across the polar plateau. In his delirium, a number of important figures from his life came to him. They walked with him and spoke to him as he hauled his sledge along. The thing is, these friends and loved ones are dead. Some had been killed while climbing in his company; some died without him being there. His mother and sister – the bright sparks of his family, who were killed in a plane crash in Nepal – walked with him during his times of deepest isolation. I brought this book along as a reference for our trek and to provide an opportunity to speak to the Boss about his life and his incredible experiences.

Sitting together in the tent the night before, I had asked him, 'Boss, just reading here about your climb on K2, Pakistan, in 1995. You are within a few hundred metres of the summit when you observe the weather begin to deteriorate. What are you able to share with us about that episode?' The Boss thinks for a moment: 'I was climbing with a group of seven others, including my very dear friend Jeff Lakes. We departed camp on what was to be summit day at 11 p.m. in the dark. We had managed to get to 26 000 feet on the summit ridge. The cold was brutal. It was –40°C.' He flicks through his book, finding the place, and begins to read aloud:

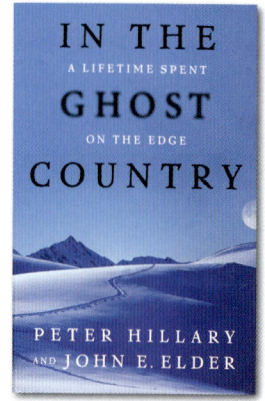

We both felt it – the cold that said 'I am going to kill you.' Our blood had turned to engine oil. We were dehydrated. We were unable to move with the sort of vigour that warms a body.

We headed down to the Spanish high camp to warm up, and we met the others in passing, as they were coming up. My teammate Bruce Grant was way out in front of the others, moving like a robot. I gave him the rope.

Bruce was a famous superman in New Zealand ... But K2 is K2, and when I gave him the rope he wasn't saying much, and he didn't look great, but he wanted to get to the top and that's where he was at.

As Alison Hargraves went by she said, 'I'm going on.' Nothing more. Eyes straight ahead.

Alison was a British climber who had just become famous for climbing Everest without oxygen and without clipping onto any of the ropes. For weeks she'd wanted to get to the top of K2 and go home to her children.

And then well below her came the already ghostly Rob Slater. Head down, resolute. 'Summit or die,' he had said before leaving the States. 'Either way I win.' He had been looking exhausted for days now.

I had the intellectual capacity of a slow six year old at this point ... I was retarded at the time. Oh, handicapped, challenged, and the rest of it. 'Retarded' works because that's how you feel. But I knew enough to say that they [Alison and Bruce] were walking simple too.

When I later told one reporter that I felt that Alison and the others had been, 'blinkered from what was developing around them and that the group chemistry seemed all wrong', it hurt people, families. In at least three countries. Then the reporter suggested, 'Did they have summit fever?' Well yes, I suppose in a way they did. And so I confirmed the media prognosis. But to know summit fever or even to have a notion of what it might be, you would have to go there yourself.

This report was picked up by newspapers everywhere. It went around the world like a bad smell. Love and truth. When they stink, they stink.

And still this hurting family, Bruce Grant's family, wanted me to tell them what happened up there, to their boy, their amazing boy. All that I could tell them with any certainty were the same things I'd already tried to tell that reporter, the bare facts of the event as I knew them, and my appraisal of what went wrong for them.

So I couldn't tell them much at all. I sat with them and looked at all the old photographs of Bruce.

The last time I talked to Bruce was when I gave him the rope. We didn't talk long. It was cold. I was very cold.

Bruce headed on up. I followed Jeff down to the Spanish camp, a few hundred feet down the shoulder.

The Boss looks up from the book, explaining that he and Jeff rested for two hours in their bags, trying to warm up with a hot brew, before going again. He reads on:

As we moved up, we could see the others. They were inching ahead, slow, hauling themselves up the bottleneck and onto the exposed traverse to the summit ridge. Hard going, clearly ...

When I got to the bottleneck, I cut a ledge in the snow and sat down in it to take a drink from my thermos and wait for [Jeff]. As I watched him come up the sloping ground I noticed there were clouds swirling over the summit. Snowflakes kept landing on my mittens. I suddenly felt it was all wrong ...

I told him that it looked bad to me, and that I was heading down ... all the way down to our happier spot at Camp Two, a drop of about five thousand feet.

I was getting wired with the whole thing. I was wired anyway. If a man was transported from the death zone, high on a mountain, to the front window of your house, you would think that a homicidal maniac was looking in at you.

That's how I would have looked ... All I could hear in my head was, 'Get down now.'

Jeff Lakes decided to go on for a while. He said he probably wouldn't keep going for too much longer, that he'd probably turn around sooner than later, but he also said that he couldn't bear the disappointment if the others got up and he missed out ... that was our last conversation.

What was Jeff thinking?

As we sat there, we heard a woman's voice calling from up above. It was Alison. 'Come on up. Use the red rope.'

Looking back to Minaret Peak from Horseshoe Valley

Jeff continued to climb, but the Boss was out of there. He reads to us now from another part of the book, describing his desperate descent to the lower camp:

> The only reason that I would wilfully travel through a white storm into crevasse country would be to escape an otherwise certain death up high.

> In fact, that was the situation on K2 for me, a desperate blind run for my life where I reversed backward down the steep face, kicking snow behind and below me so I had some guide as to where to place my feet.

> If it tumbled and stopped somewhere below me, I put my foot on that spot where the shadow of the clump of snow was cast. In the white on white world of the storm it was difficult to see the snowball. If it seemed to disappear, then I assumed the ground fell away there and I'd deviate across the face and kick the snow in a new direction. At one point, when I did my little mule kick to send off another snowball to scout the way into the white oblivion, the entire slope broke loose for several yards in every direction. Perched upon a rambling carpet of rapidly descending snow, I shot down the face. It was steep country. I wasn't on a rope.

The Boss looks up again from his book. 'I thought that was it,' he tells us. 'I clawed at the slope and skipped over a crevasse, sliding for seconds that seemed like minutes before managing to get my ice axe and crampon spikes to grip on the face of the slope. I wanted to scream for help but instinctively knew that none could come. I resumed kicking the snowballs down and finding my footholds. It was the storm born of the clouds that I had seen swirling around the summit earlier. I had tried to outrun it but it was coming up the mountain like a thousand freight trains. People later said what an unusual storm it was, climbing up the mountain like that. It went all the way to the top.

'I got into the tent at the lower camp absolutely spent and tried to warm up. To my absolute surprise, Jeff rappelled down to us a day later in the middle of the night. We tried to fill him with warm tea, which he drank instinctively, but he never spoke. He died in his bag later that day.' Again the Boss picks up his book and reads to us:

> I just remember coming off our route and into base camp, and what remained of the Spanish group were coming off their route, staggering in, looking appalling, and everyone just absolutely out of it, and we followed them in. You staggered

TRAVEL ROUTE

HERITAGE RANGE

HORSESHOE VALLEY

High Nunatak
1310M

Moulder Pk
1868M

Sponholz Pk
1730M

Kelley Pk
1710M

ELLSWORTH MOUNTAINS

CAMP 3

CAMP 4

Crevasse
field

CAMP 2

Minaret Pk
1613M

Mt Fordell
1670M

Mt Simmons
1590M

CAMP 1

Crash site
DC-6

PATRIOT HILLS
CAMP
Blue ice runway

Patriot Hills
1246M

N

SCALE

0   20   40   60 KILOMETRES

MOUNTAIN
RANGE

CREVASSE

DAY TRIP 1

DAY TRIP 2

MAIN TREK

through their camp, and you knew that half of the Spanish were dead. You staggered through the American camp, and you knew all of them were dead. You arrived at our camp, and you knew that half of them were dead. So, yeah, you got in there and had all these cups of tea and went to bed.

I recall reading a magazine article that the Boss had written about this ill-fated climb on K2, in which he describes what his climbing companions would have faced higher up on K2. The following passage is burnt deep into my memory: 'Imagine being in a huge industrial freezer at –40. You are hooked onto a rope with your harness and ascenders. Now get a 747 jet engine and turn it on to full blast, shooting its freezing air into you. Now tilt the freezer to an angle of almost vertical. Now turn out the light!' K2 is clearly not on my must-do list.

Now as I ski across the snow and ice, I think about what is important to me. I think about how privileged I am to be here with two great friends exploring this frozen wonderland. I dream of my family in Australia and how beautifully warm it must be back there. Mum and Dad. My sister and her family. I think about Caroline and young Florence, who appear on the side of the track to cheer me on from time to time. I am not hallucinating, just imagining them here with me. Or maybe I am hallucinating; maybe I have been talking to the Boss too much. I think about the members of Scott's expedition, stuck in this country, freezing and starving to death. I think about heroic Oates in particular: 'I am just going outside and may be some time.' I think about Mawson describing the continent as 'this accursed land.' I know why we are here. We are moving through a land unlike anything that I could have possibly imagined. One of Arthur C. Clarke's observations keeps ringing in my head: 'Sometimes I think we're alone in the universe, and sometimes I think we're not. In either case the idea is quite staggering.'

At 80 degrees south, nothing lives. Lichen cannot grow on rocks. You do not even see an errant bird blown off course. It is just you, your companions and the hostile elements to test you. Life here is as different as life on another planet. Everything is foreign, yet oddly familiar. You see the sun, but it never sets. You see the moon but never the stars. You feel the sun, but it does not warm you. You see clouds, but it never rains. I can talk to Caroline every day but never see her. Life in the freezer is odd – and invigorating.

We break for lunch and put on our down jackets the instant we stop moving. Setting up for a lunch break in poor weather is a challenge. This involves the very amusing and very difficult task of getting three grown men to stand together in a triangle facing each other so that we can slip a tiny 'bivvy bag' the size of a large laundry bag over all our heads and shuffle it down to our bums before attempting to sit down smoothly and slowly. Amid much groaning and laughter, we finally get it organised. My head is no further than 30 centimetres from my companions' faces as I struggle for a moderately comfortable position within the small sack.

Once inside and settled it is wonderful to be out of the wind, even if it is only for half an hour. Thermos flasks are found; instant soup and noodles are broken out. A hot drink within minutes of sitting down is an absolute treat. Our cramped little bag has become a den of delight. Mertz asks the Boss, 'Who is the best polar traveller in the world?' Without hesitation, he replies, 'Børge Ousland, the Norwegian. Those Norwegians really know about polar travel. Børge is truly a remarkable fellow; in 1990 he was the first man to ski to the North Pole without supply drops; in 1994 he was the first to ski solo to the North Pole again without supply drops; in 1995 he skied solo to the South Pole, in 1996 he traversed Greenland as a warm-up for his solo ski later that year. Later in 1996 he would ski solo across Antarctica via the South Pole covering the 2845 kilometres in just 64 days. The man is a phenomenon. More recently in 2001 he crossed the Arctic from Siberia to Canada via the North Pole in 82 days, and in 2003 he completed the first unsupported traverse of the Patagonian ice cap by kayak, skis and sledge. I would love to meet him one day. He is the one. Without doubt the worlds pre-eminent polar traveller.'

Børge Ousland – we would love to meet him too.

Before long, Mertz's leg begins to cramp and he needs to move his large frame about in order to get settled again. I get out the snack bags that I prepared with Caroline in Australia. They are a triumph, consisting of dried apricots, died apples, coconut shavings, chocolate, cashews, almonds, dried peas, jelly snakes, 'strawberries and cream' jubes, and pine nuts. There is a communal groan as we lift the bivvy bag and the wind rips through us.

We had been hauling for more than four hours before our lunch stop. The decision is made to head towards Minaret Peak. Mertz and the Boss commend me on my work leading the group that morning. I decide that I am feeling good and will keep pushing along from the front. After an hour or so I look back to see the others a few hundred metres behind me, and, perhaps feeling a little overconfident, I take it upon myself to turn left up the ridge protecting Minaret Peak. Now my skis are removed and fastened securely to the sledge, which balances beautifully behind me. I signal across the ridge to the Boss and Mertz that I am taking a direct course towards Minaret Peak. They both swing up the ridge and follow.

As we push up the ridge, we are forced to zigzag back and forth as the ground is too steep to ascend directly. The shoulder straps of my backpack dig in and tear at my shoulders as I

lean into the slope with the fully-laden sledge following reluctantly behind. This zigzagging goes on for more than an hour before I finally crest the ridge and see Minaret Peak close up for the first time. It is now three hours since the lunch break and almost eight since we broke camp. I am still feeling quite strong. There is no time to gawk or photograph as a blast of wind almost knocks me over. Head down, I push with my legs into a fierce wind that is blowing 40 knots and gusting up to 60. The wind is so strong through this section that the blue ice is revealed in large patches ahead. My crampons should be on now to help me grip the blue ice, but I am enjoying the challenge of walking without them on the slick, windswept surface. The crampons are in the top of my pack if things get really nasty.

We are headed into the jaws of a particularly fierce katabatic blow. I am working very hard, which keeps me warm. I check the temperature gauge: it has seized up at –30°c; the wind is still knocking me around at 40 knots and gusting 80 knots. I pause to consider the wind chill. Wind chill measures the rate of heat loss from the skin that is exposed to wind. As wind speed increases, heat loss from the skin also increases, which in turn makes the passing air feel colder. Take, for instance, the current temperature at approximately –30°c. In still conditions, the wind-chill temperature will be the same as the actual temperature. Under these conditions, my skin will begin to freeze in 20–30 minutes. But when you factor in the steady 40 knots that I am walking into, the wind chill is roughly –50°c. I become fascinated with wind chill. It is a wonderful way to exaggerate the hardships we are enduring. At this temperature, any exposed skin will begin to freeze (causing frostbite) within 5–10 minutes. The spindrift continues to blast me from all sides. It is bloody freezing!

I look back to see Mertz coming up behind me, with the Boss further back still. At this point I am considering my options: wait for the others so that we can confer on our campsite – it's too cold to stop – or push on and hope for a campsite to become apparent, soon! I decide to push on into the wind, with Minaret Peak towering above me. An odd thing happens when approaching a peak: it seems so close that you can touch it, but it is very difficult to cover the ground to get there. Four or five times I tell myself that I will be there in less than an hour. It is now more than five hours since the lunch break and ten hours since we broke camp this morning. My legs begin to slow, the colds bites deeper. There are now only tiny patches of snow on the blue ice on which to get a decent grip while walking. Remaining steady is difficult, but the sledge really does roar along this blue ice with minimal hauling.

As I approach the base of Minaret Peak, I look back to see the Boss and Mertz engaged in animated conversation. They are both attending to their sledges. All of a sudden, a long item is whipped up by the wind, lifted from one of their sledges, and begins to dance across the blue ice. Mertz, wearing his crampons, sprints across the blue ice like a startled gazelle, chasing the unidentified item. The item miraculously lays itself flat for a few seconds, allowing Mertz to leap upon it. What a brilliant save! They move on, but they are no longer following me to Minaret Peak; instead they are edging along the blue ice and away from my target destination. Now Mertz is coming towards me without his sledge. I suspect that he is the bearer of a message from the Boss. By the time Mertz arrives, I have just finished surveying the base of Minaret Peak for a campsite, but there is nothing suitable. I begin to get the feeling that I have led the group into a dead end.

Mertz arrives with the following news: 'The Boss is not happy, Oates! He almost lost his mat – you may have noticed me dash across the ice after it. He has been blown over by the katabatic a few times. To quote him directly: "Where the blooming hell is Oates going? This has turned into an epic!" Oates, you had better put those crampons on ol' mate and get over here.'

Morraines at the base of Minaret Peak

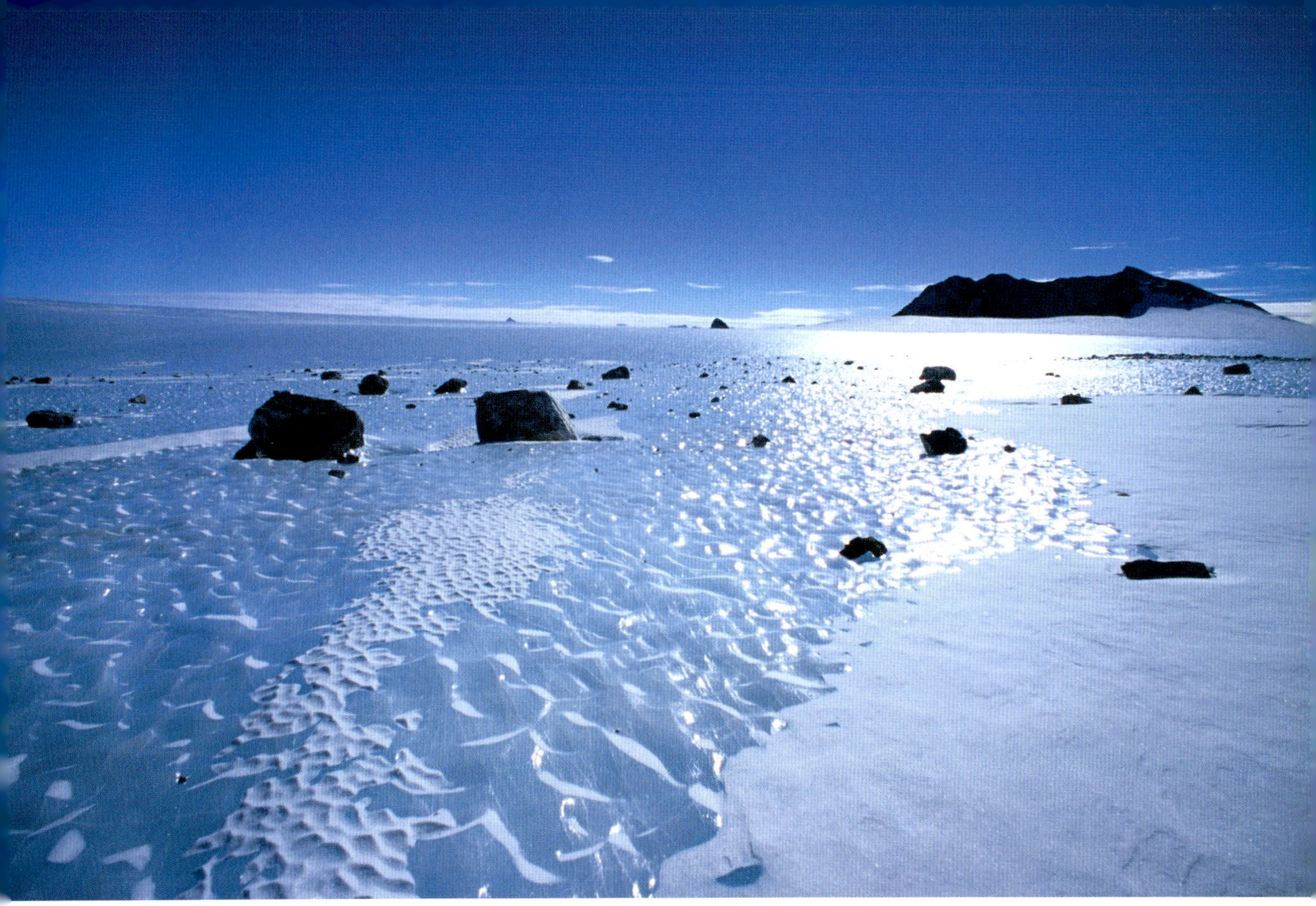

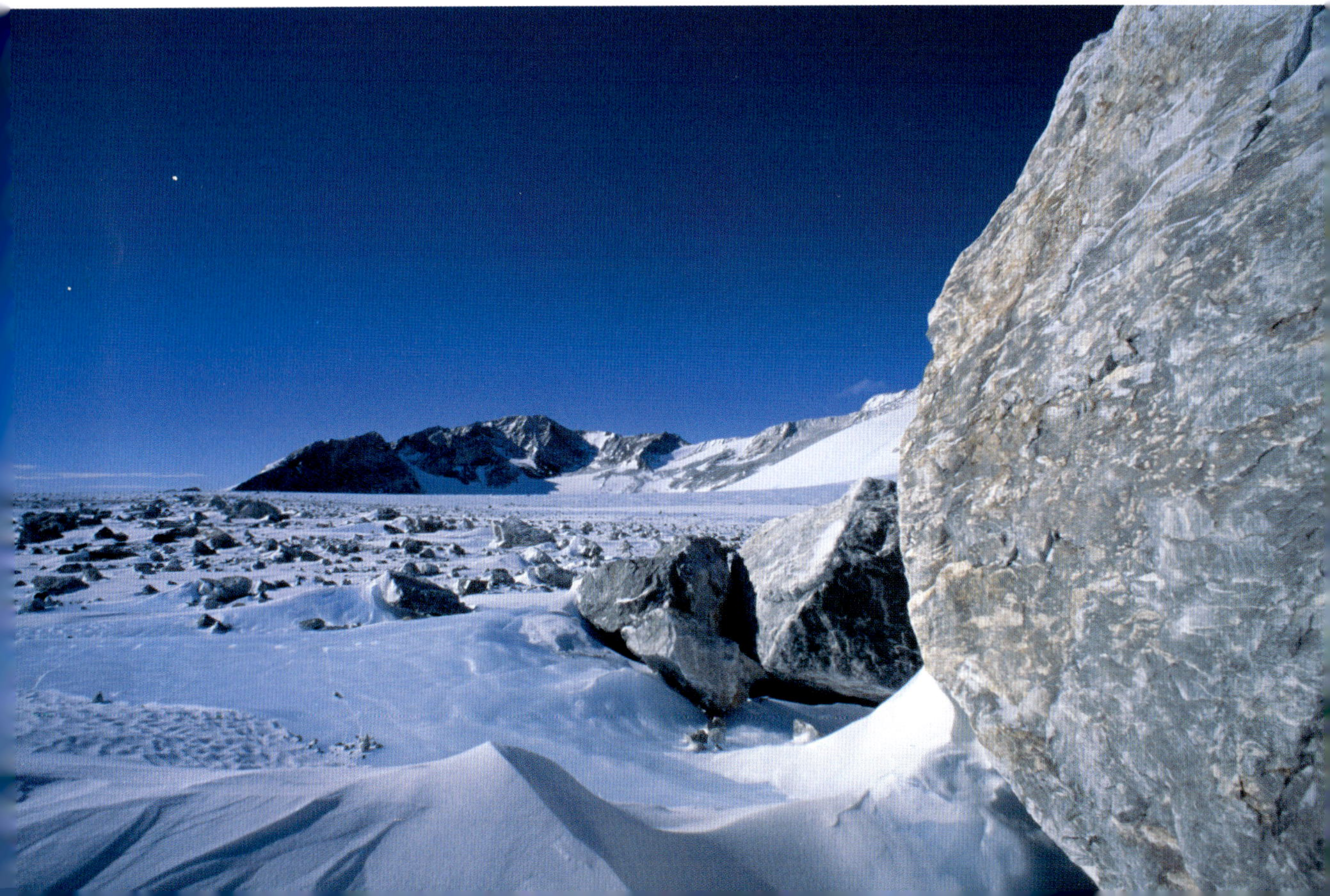

Oops? It sounds like the Boss is very unhappy with me. Thankfully he has vented his frustration with Mertz and has cooled off considerably by the time I get over to him.

'Oates, where the hell are you going?'

I have a quick think. 'Minaret?'

'Yes, but there is no place to fix a tent here – look at this place.' He does have a point. The area is nothing but solid blue ice and a few moraines (lone rocks that sit atop the ice fields, having been ripped off the mountain by the katabatic's force). The view to the south is straight up Minaret Peak; to the east lies the ridge line of the Marble Hills. The wind is howling down the slopes, threatening to sit us all on our bums again.

'Boss, I thought that we wanted to get to Minaret,' I offer, hoping to diffuse the building tension.

'Yes, but not with our last steps. This has turned into a bloody epic. You have to stop, consider and discuss these things, Oates. It's been a very tough day. We have been going for over twelve hours now in positively brutal conditions.'

Blue ice fields

Minaret Peak

Minaret Peak

You have really done it now, Oates! I try to think of a response, deciding that 'guilty as charged' is the only approach available to me.

'Apologies, Boss, I should have stopped and checked on everyone.'

'Definitely, Oates. Now let's find a place for these tents.' Needless to say, this exchange is peppered with plenty of appalling language – omitted here for the sake of the delicate.

I look for positives in the search for a campsite. There are none. The Boss suggests a shift across the ridge, which will mean another two hours' hauling – a prospect that does not appeal in the slightest. We are here now; let's make the best of it. The location is as spectacular as it is inhospitable. I head instinctively for the biggest moraine and suggest that we get in behind it with the tents. After much humming, arrghing and gnashing of teeth, it is decided to erect tents here at the foot of Minaret Peak. It will be no easy task.

This will be our only camp pitched directly on the blue ice. Well, I say directly on the ice, but there are a couple of centimetres of crusty old icy snow that we manage to drag onto the tent site. It is impossible to build a snow wall of any description, as everything around us is frozen solid. Tonight we will be forced to rely on the large moraine for protection from the katabatic. I manage to hack off a few loose chunks of ice for melting with my ice axe before slipping into the tent to get some water on the boil. We are all spent after a long and onerous thirteen-hour day of hauling. The Boss and Mertz are outside for over an hour fixing ice screws into the blue ice and tying the tents down onto the surrounding moraines.

I have hot drinks ready for them as they shimmy into the tent and into their sleeping bags. It is more than twenty minutes until anyone can speak. The Boss speaks first: 'Gentlemen, I don't like how we got here, but we have an absolutely amazing camp.' We all drink to this. You have to shout to be heard above the wind blasting past. The Boss estimates the gusts to be in excess of 100 kilometres per hour and shares his concerns for the security of the tents. The sun disappears behind Minaret Peak, leaving us in the shade for the first time since we arrived in Antarctica. There is a sense of something precarious about this campsite.

The temperature plummets. It has become very, very cold. At least –40°c now without the 'warming sunlight'. I am in my down-filled sleeping bag wearing my long johns, thermal pants, down pants, long johns top, polar fleece top, jacket, beanie, two pairs of socks and my tent boots.

As we lie in the tent reading about the Boss's tribulations on his 72-day trek to the South Pole, the wind begins to drop considerably. This is a pleasant relief at first. The howl of the wind, however, is replaced with the unnerving pop of the ice cracking beneath us. It is the sound of ice cubes being dropped in a glass of water. 'Pop! Pop! Pop! Pop! Pop! Pop! Pop! Pop!' The first few are a little scary, but I soon get used to the sound, and eventually it becomes like friendly chatter beneath me.

Chapter 7

CREVASSE COUNTRY

We spend a very cold night at Minaret Peak. In the morning we are reluctant to get out of the tent, so we don't. The pots are simmering, the food and drinks hot. The pee bottle is nearby. We are enjoying an in-depth debrief and reminisce about yesterday's epic. It is a lot funnier today. All is forgiven, and laughed about – very loudly! After briefly reminding me what a mug I was for pushing on without consultation, the Boss is now raving about how magnificent the camp is under Minaret Peak and how lucky we are to be here. My vindication is complete.

We are all chatting in the tent, enjoying a hot brew, when the subject turns to Antarctic travel and reaching the South Pole. Most people are aware of the great race between Scott and Amundsen of 1911 and 1912, but very few people know that the next successful attempt to reach the South Pole took place some 46 years later, in 1958. A man with three farm tractors, who wasn't even meant to be at the South Pole, achieved this. His name is Sir Edmund Hillary. I cannot help but think that conquering the South Pole has a similar history to that of the lunar landings of the late 1960s and early '70s. Both missions started out as impossible dreams before bursting onto the international stage in a wave of media hype. Each of them brought together curious novelty, national fanfare, fierce competition and high levels of public interest before rapidly fading to a distant memory in the public consciousness. In both cases, there seemed to be a general feeling of 'That's done now. What's next?' We are such fickle creatures, us humans. I digress.

In 1956, Sir Edmund Hillary was invited to join the very English Antarctic veteran Dr Vivian Fuchs on his British Trans-Antarctic Expedition. Using mechanical Sno-Cats, Fuchs planned to cross the continent from the Atlantic side to the Pacific side via the South Pole with the aim of becoming the fastest ever to reach the pole, the first to get there by going overland for 46 years, the third man ever to reach the pole and the first man to cross the continent.

Sir Edmund Hillary on the New Zealand five dollar note

Ed Hillary was to come from the Pacific side, laying fuel and food depots for Fuchs to use once he had reached the pole and had begun his final leg of the journey towards the Pacific. Hillary had served the British well on Everest in 1953, and it was thought that he would obediently do what the British required of him again. Hillary was making different plans.

With his three modified Massey Ferguson farm tractors, Ed Hillary made tremendous progress, weaving through crevasse fields and setting up all the depots for Fuchs exactly as instructed. Meanwhile, on the other side of the continent, Fuchs was struggling to progress as quickly with his high-tech Sno-Cats and was carrying out all manner of experiments along the way, proving, for instance, that Antarctica is in fact a large land mass and not a huge lump of ice.

As Ed Hillary got closer and closer to the pole, Fuchs started getting apprehensive about his colleague's proximity to the pole, sending via radio a flurry of extra and unnecessary instructions and tasks for Hillary to carry out before proceeding. At this point, Hillary and his team of four – known as the 'Old Firm' – were 700 miles from their base at McMurdo, with a further 500 miles to the pole. To really put the wind up Fuchs, Hillary sent a press release to the world media on Boxing Day 1957: 'Am hell bent for the Pole, God willing and crevasse permitting.'

Fuchs by now was very apprehensive about being gazumped, sending further instructions for Ed Hillary and the Old Firm to carry out. Not to be outdone, Hillary completed them all and moved towards the pole. They pushed on until the pole was within sight. Their position was recorded, and the world waited to hear from Hillary as to what his next move would be. The British press were already going batty at the thought of a New Zealander, no less, taking the glory that was due to the British and that had been coveted since Amundsen pipped Scott back in 1911. From the passionate way the Boss tells this story about his father, you get the feeling that Ed Hillary is a real character, a bit of a colonial boy and not adverse to standing up to the Brits – a favourite pastime of most Antipodeans.

So, within sight of the pole, Hillary was due to radio in to base. Fuchs, the British media and all of the support bases in Antarctica were listening in at the prescribed time, ready for a long, drawn-out explanation of why Hillary will or will not go for the pole the next day. The radio crackled to life, and you could almost feel everyone lean forward to be the first to hear this historic radio message. Hillary and his men had been in deep conversation for many hours deciding on what to say when the time came. The message having been composed, Peter Mulgrew was nominated to deliver it. The radio was ready. The message was sent: 'Rhubarb!' With that he switched the radio off and all the Old Firm fell about the floor of their tent laughing. You can only imagine the look on Fuchs' face when the news reached him.

Hillary and the Old Firm rolled into the recently built US Amundsen/Scott base at the South Pole the next day, 4 January 1958, the third party to ever to reach the pole by travelling overland from the coast and some two weeks ahead of Fuchs. It wasn't all bad news for Fuchs though: he did manage to complete the crossing of the continent and was knighted for his efforts. Ed Hillary had planned his dash to the pole all along and was delighted to have executed his plan so smoothly. The Boss tells this story with great pride and passion. My admiration for Ed Hillary has just gone up another rung.

We decide that it is time to do some exploring of our own, so despite the relentless winds and freezing temperatures we get ready for a short day trip around Minaret Peak. We wriggle out of the tent only to get blown down by the fierce katabatic. We have to shout at each other to be heard. It is unwise to stop and hang about for too long as the cold begins to bite hard. Today is a day for balaclava, facemask, hat, four layers of clothing, two pairs of socks, goggles, ice axe, crampons and your sense of humour. We walk up the nearby ridge and around the camp in a wide arc before passing Minaret Peak for a view of the polar plateau rising up beneath us.

Day trip at Minaret Peak

Mertz and the Boss sillhouetted on blue ice

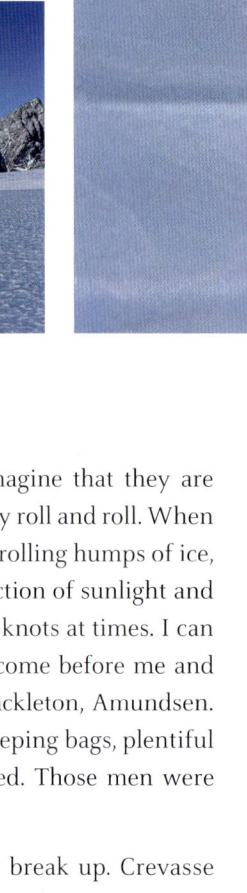

The blue ice fields surround us like surging waves on the ocean. I imagine that they are capable of turning to liquid and crashing down on us at any moment. They roll and roll. When I stand back to observe the Boss and Mertz walking up one of these huge rolling humps of ice, it is not difficult to imagine that they are walking on water with its reflection of sunlight and smooth motion. The wind is blowing at 40 knots and gusting at up to 60 knots at times. I can feel the heat being drained out of my body. I think of those who have come before me and the hardships they endured – Oates, Mertz, Ninnis, Mawson, Scott, Shackleton, Amundsen. We, on the other hand, can simply hike back to the tent with its down sleeping bags, plentiful supplies, fuel for afternoon tea – we can even radio for help if required. Those men were isolated, alone, with death slowly constricting them.

As we climb over the hummock, the icy ground beneath us begins to break up. Crevasse field! Code red! When huge sheets of ice move over a hump, hill or hummock, or even over a

boulder, they crack and open up, forming a crevasse. They can be hundreds of metres deep, so we are very careful to stay on the 'blue bits'. It's like when you are a child and you avoid stepping on the lines in the footpath so as not to be attacked by an invisible bear or some other imaginary creature. My memory races back to childhood, and I remember going for years at a time without stepping on a line. This is a very encouraging recollection – I have the ability to avoid danger.

The 'blue bits' are the pinnacles of the massive ice towers on which we are walking. These towers slowly move over the ground below. The white bits are where drifts of snow have blown in between the cracks, forming snow bridges that can range from a couple of centimetres to several metres thick. These snow bridges give the untrained eye the false impression that they are safe to walk over. Nothing could be further from the truth. A snow bridge can collapse without warning at any time. Stick to the blue! Steer clear of the white!

After about four hours of relentless buffeting, Mertz and I begin to tire and start wandering out of the crevasse field and back towards camp, closely followed by the Boss. We are both weary, and with our concentration waning we walk directly into a crevasse. The feeling that rushes over me as I begin to disappear into the crevasse is more than a little disconcerting but I am pleasantly surprised at how quickly we thrust out our arms and swing our ice axes into the blue ice for a rapid arrest.

The Boss, Mertz and I head back to the tents. Mertz has been rattled by his crevasse experience as his diary attests: 'Crevasse fields – they are scary. I jumped over a crevasse today and broke the snow bridge as I landed on the other side. I looked down into the dark blue abyss. I am terrified of crevasses. I do not want to be within a kilometre of them. They instil the worst fear imaginable.'

Back in the tent we plan our route to return to Horseshoe Valley tomorrow. It will involve retracing our steps and avoiding the crevasse field to the north. The Boss expresses some interest in winding around the crevasse field to find a new route and roping up for safety. Understandably, Mertz has no interest in this proposal.

That night we get updates from Patriot Hills on the progress of the other groups. The climbing teams at Mount Vinson have been pinned down at camp two for three days by strong winds. One tent has been shredded and the occupants forced to build an ice cave for shelter. There are more than twenty climbers who are unable to leave their tents at this camp. The British expedition travelling in the converted Ford is making good progress. They have done a fuel drop 300 kilometres out from the Patriot Hills base and have returned safely. They will depart tomorrow for their dash to the South Pole. There have been no further Ilyushin flights since the one that came in the day after we arrived. The weather has been too poor. We all agree that we are very happy with our decision to trek rather than climb. The Boss has calculated that the group at camp two on Vinson will be experiencing –40°C owing to the altitude and the wind patterns that have been reported in the region. Leave me out of it!

The Minaret Peak camp takes almost three hours to pack up and load onto the sledges. The ice screws that have secured the tent for the past two days prove difficult to remove. It is again bitterly cold and windy. We are all wearing our crampons for the long haul across the blue ice before we reach the snow-crusted valley floor. I am caught unawares as the Boss scoots to the front and seeks to take the alternative route that I thought Mertz and I had put the kybosh on the previous evening. Go Boss! This could get exciting. Mertz will not be happy. We roll over and across the smooth humps of ice as we work our way along the ridge. All is going beautifully for the minute. I crane my neck to see what lies ahead. The ground is clearly breaking up – crevasses!

Departing Minaret Peak

CREVASSE
CROSS SECTION

We now find ourselves in the crevasse field. At first the crevasses are very narrow – hairline cracks in the blue ice beneath us. These cracks begin to open appreciably until we are forced to pick our way through them. Movement in a straight line is impossible; our journey has just turned into a serious game of snakes and ladders, and my next step could be my last. We are not roped up.

The Boss leads, I follow him, and Mertz follows me. I am beginning to feel that burst of exhilaration that I felt climbing along the icy volcanic lip of Mount Ruapehu. With mixed emotions of imminent danger and pure excitement, the knowledge that any mistake in this place will be costly is somewhat sobering. It is hard to explain this thrill other than to say that as long as you are in control of your own destiny, the closer you come to the possibility of death, the more exciting life becomes. It is important to maintain mental and physical control, both of yourself and of the situation, in order to appreciate the excitement that comes with this knife-edge predicament.

The crevasses are getting wider now, over a metre in many parts, and it seems as if we are trapped in a giant maze with no apparent exit. I keep trying new routes but often come to dead ends. The blue ice is like concrete. As I cross a snow bridge, it suddenly collapses behind me under the weight of the trailing sledge. The sledge slips into the crevasse, slamming into the crevasse wall and threatening to pull me in with it. I quickly brace myself, leaning forward to counterbalance the strain in the rope. Thankfully my crampons' grip on the ice is firm and I am able to pull the sledge gradually up and out. Mertz, who is still behind me, is unnerved by what he has just witnessed.

Beginning of the crevasse field

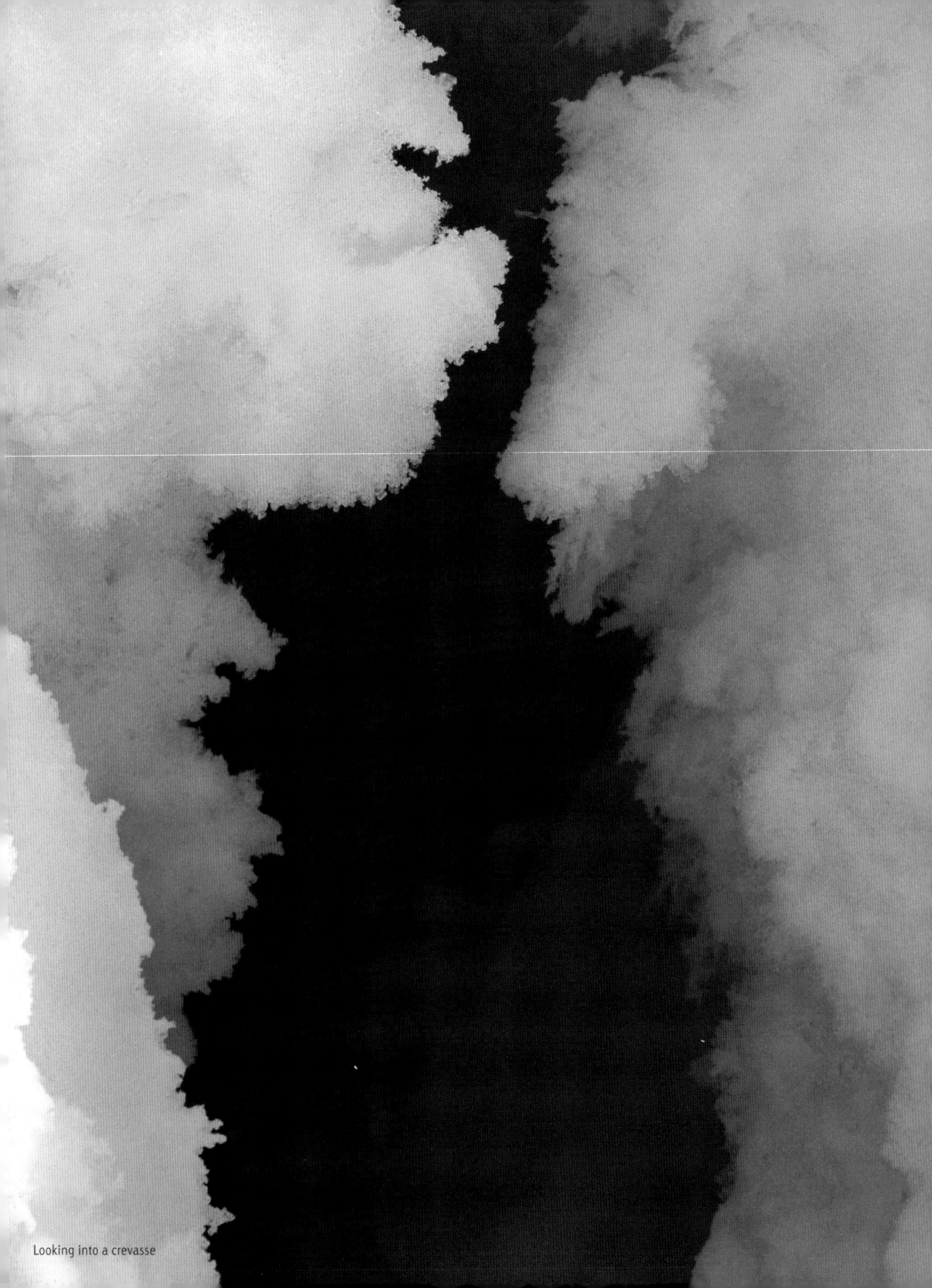

Looking into a crevasse

'How are you going, Mertz?' No response. 'Mertz, Mertz!' I turn back to see my companion poking his ski pole through an ice bridge to reveal a bottomless crevasse beneath. It is quite clear that he is freaking himself out. 'Mertz!'

'Sorry, mate, but I am not enjoying this at all. Let's get the hell out of this bloody crevasse field. You know how clumsy I am – this is not the place for me.' I reassure him that everything is all right and that we are heading out of the crevasse field.

'Not soon enough!'

The Boss pushes on out front, followed by me and then Mertz at the rear. I am finding it exciting but my thoughts are interrupted by Mertz screaming. 'Boss, Oates, we said that we should speak up if we are unhappy or uncomfortable! Well I am speaking up! Unhappy *and* uncomfortable! Get me out of here now, and rope me up immediately!' With that I call ahead to the Boss, who, like me, is positively thriving on the situation. 'Boss, Mertz is very unhappy. We need to get out of here now.' The Boss acquiesces and changes course by 100 degrees so that we can haul our sledges directly out of the crevasse field. It is –35°C, and the wind is steady at 40 knots. This puts the wind chill at approximately –50°C, with a high risk of frostbite to any exposed skin in 5–10 minutes.

I leave the crevasses behind with more than a little sadness. Once we are clear of the danger zone, we do a gear inspection to assess any damage to the sledges. I lift up the nose of my sledge to find a hole the size of a large melon in the middle of the front section. This must have occurred when it slammed into the ice wall before almost pulling me in. The Boss also has a hole in his sledge, as does Mertz. But mine is the biggest – a badge of honour or a tag of stupidity? Needless to say, Mertz is thrilled to be leaving the 'horrid crevasse country', as it will become known.

It takes us four hours, but we finally make it down from Minaret Peak and safely onto the valley floor. It is time for a lunch break in the hysterical bivvy bag that protects us from the elements – but not each other. We gather the required gear and stand face to face; the bag

Photographer: P. Hillary

Photographer: P. Hillary

is placed over the top of our heads and tugged down to our knees before a group shimmy ensues, taking us all the way down to the ground. The result is a tangle of legs and boots inside the tiny bivvy bag.

'Oh wait, that's my leg. Sorry, no, it's yours.'

'Hey, can you get off my lunch?'

'Where is my thermos? Here, can you pass it?'

'Thermos coming through. Got it?'

'Clear!'

Eating lunch in this bivvy bag is like playing Twister in a oversized condom. Pouring the boiling water for our soups only increases the degree of difficulty. Mertz begins to cramp first, and we all bend and stretch to accommodate his movements as he attempts to regain the blood flow to his leg. It is more slapstick vaudeville than lunch. Afterwards, the bivvy bag is lifted off and the temperature plummets 40°c from 10°c to −30°c. Invigorating to say the least.

With lunch finished and the bivvy bag packed away until next time, we trek north along Horseshoe Valley for a few hours. We are moving briskly up the valley with the Liberty Hills to our left and the High Nunatak directly ahead. I am leading the group, with the Boss and Mertz only a few metres behind. Suddenly my sledge feels much lighter, and I assume this is because I have just skied over a small hill and am hauling the sledge downhill. But it continues to feel light ... Perhaps my energy and strength have improved. I power ahead, relishing my newfound strength. Mertz and the Boss break into laughter as I turn around to find that I am pulling only the front third of the sledge, with no load. It's broken in two. Little wonder it had become such easy hauling. Amid much mirth at my expense, we declare that this will be the camp for the night: camp three, directly beneath Kelley Peak.

Photographer: P. Hillary   Smashed sledge

Chapter 8

SNOW STORM
AT HIGH NUNATAK

With the adventures of the crevasse behind us, we are happily setting up camp three under Kelley Peak. Following the normal procedure, Mertz assists me with the snow wall while the Boss erects the tents. Once this is all done, I retire to the tent to prepare hot drinks and get dinner underway. This quiet time in the tent is one of the more amusing aspects of the trip as I get to listen to the Boss and Mertz go about their business. The Boss is very well schooled in Antarctic travel, having been on ten expeditions, including to the summit of Mount Vinson and the horrific 72-day man-hauling trek to the South Pole, and is careful and cautious with the tents and our equipment. Mertz, as I have noted, is a little heavy-handed and prone to accidents. These two always finish securing the tent together while I am inside preparing the hot drinks. They always have plenty to chatter about.

'Ah, Boss, have you seen the shovel?'

'Yes, Mertz, just at the tent door.'

'Got it!'

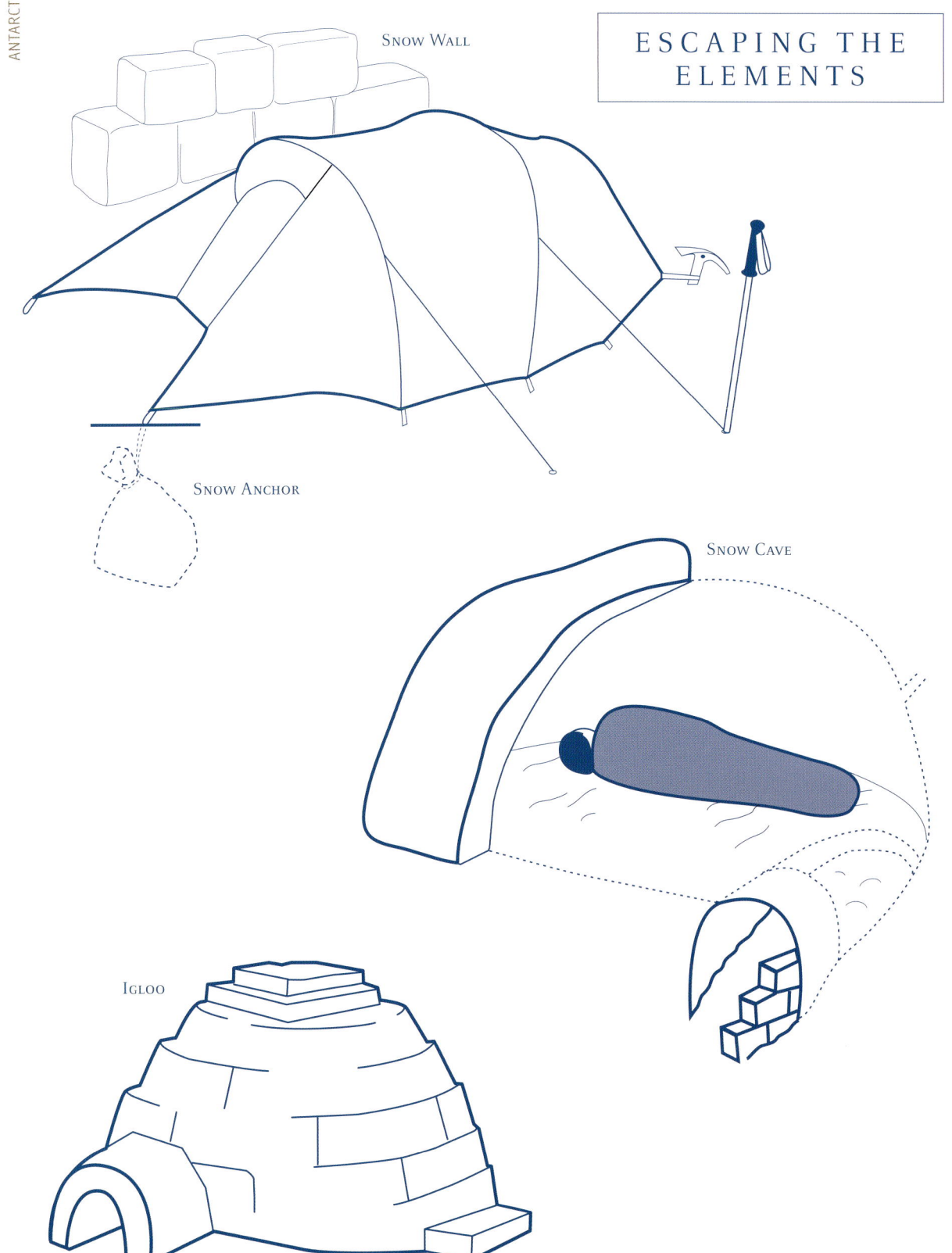

Snow Wall

ESCAPING THE
ELEMENTS

Snow Anchor

Snow Cave

Igloo

The Boss invariably finds an inexplicable knot or hitch when securing the guy ropes, and rather than accusing Mertz of heavy-handedness, he makes a general announcement: 'What on earth is happening here?'

'Everything all right, Boss?' Mertz asks.

'It is just that I cannot understand this curious knot.' Translation: 'Jeepers, Mertz, what have you done to my guy ropes?' A little fed up with being held responsible for most of the damage to our equipment, Mertz bursts around to the other side of the tent to confront the Boss and his problem with the curious knot.

'Oh Boss, it just seems to have slipped around a bit in the wind. Let me fix it.'

'I am just curious as to how it got like that.' Translation: 'Mertz, I truly cannot understand what the hell you have done to my guy ropes!' I am about to burst out laughing from inside the tent, but I hold it in, not wanting to interrupt the banter. A few minutes pass before the Boss's next announcement.

'Jeepers, we are going to have to be more careful when digging the tent out of the snow. There is a shovel tear in the side of the tent fly.' Gold! Absolute gold, Boss! Translation: 'Mertz, you are destroying the fly of my tent with that bloody rough work on the shovel.'

'Impossible! Boss, I have been incredibly diligent with the shovel when digging anywhere near the tent.' Translation: 'Bloody hell! I haven't, have I?'

I hear more shuffling as Mertz comes around for a closer inspection. There is much umming and ahing as the tear in the tent fly is further examined. The Boss comes to the conclusion that there can be only one cause of the tear – Mertz! Watching him handle delicate items is like watching an elephant holding a teacup. Mertz is thoroughly entertaining, always reliable, very funny and completely loyal, and I love him dearly for it. You could not wish to travel with a better man.

The Boss and Mertz now set to work repairing the damaged and (in my case) smashed sledges. They decide that they will drill new holes through the back end of each sledge and reattach the towropes so that the sledges can be hauled backwards. This all goes smoothly.

I call Caroline on the satellite phone and give her the rundown for my website, which is updated daily with news of the trek for those who are following our progress from around the world. As I tell her about our sledges, I can think of three people are going to be very excited about this news: Mum, Dad and my father-in-law Ian. I know what their collective reaction will be: 'I told you those sledges are no good! How could you have taken them? Why didn't you get better ones? I told you that they looked very lightweight. I am not surprised. Why wouldn't you spend more money on a sledge? Why would Hillary let you take those flimsy plastic things?'

Photographer: J. Veale

Photographer: P. Hillary

Photographer: J. Veale

Photographer: J. Veale

Photographer: P. Hillary

Sponholz Peak

Photographer: P. Hillary

Kelley Peak

Sure enough, the next day I speak with Caroline and she relays the predicted response on behalf of my parents and father-in-law, almost word for word. It's funny how you instinctively know who cares about you and how they will express their love.

After being stuck in the tent for more than 24 hours due to the appalling conditions, we decide that we need to get out for some exercise, so we go for a walk. The katabatic is blowing down off the polar plateau at a moderate 20 knots, and the skies are covered in cloud. We are heading towards the High Nunatak, 12 kilometres away. This is to be a short walk in Horseshoe Valley – just for fun – so we carry only one pack between us and haul no sledges. The low cloud cover means that it's not too cold. In fact conditions are almost pleasant as we depart camp three for a leisurely walk up the valley.

After three hours walking and having covered 11 kilometres, we reach the foot of the High Nunatak. There is some light-hearted discussion about climbing the sheer face that presents itself before us, but this talk is quickly dismissed as irrational in light of the storm that seems to be moving in across the valley. The spindrift has blown up to waist height. It gets in everywhere. Like sand in the desert, it is everywhere. Any pocket that is not closed properly will fill with spindrift; a camera bag is filled via a break in its zipper. Visibility is down to 50 metres; the wind is up to 40 knots, and the temperature has just plummeted to –25°C. It has begun to snow heavily. We set our return course for camp three.

The only visible features are the top of Minaret Peak and the High Nunatak behind us. Camp three is somewhere between the two, three hours away in the distance. So after three hours of plugging away, walking directly into the katabatic, I think we must be there. I am 'seeing' the tent every few minutes now and starting to go a little batty. Visibility is now down to less than 30 metres and finding the campsite is rapidly becoming a needle-in-a-haystack job. We all fan out to give ourselves a better chance of locating the tents. A better chance! If we don't find the tents, we will quite possibly freeze to death.

Everything is white now, with occasional glimpses of Minaret Peak our only point of reference. What if the bearings are wrong? What if we get separated? What if we can't find the bloody tents? What if ...? We trudge on and on through the great white everywhere. Finally, three and a half hours after setting out from High Nunatak, Mertz spots the tents. What eagle eyes! Where would we be without Mertz?

The tents are buried in snow and spindrift, and we almost walk past them. Our afternoon sojourn has turned into a seven-hour trek, with the last two hours being particularly nerve-wracking in miserable conditions.

On arriving at the tent door, I foolishly remove my gloves before getting inside and try to dust off the spindrift that has settled in the tent's entrance. I zip the door up behind me. I move inside the tent and begin to unzip the join in the middle to gain access to the other

tent; again the zippers are covered in spindrift, which falls onto my fingers and hands. The annexe between the tents has filled with this spindrift, and it gets all over me as I pass through. My unprotected hands are again covered in spindrift, and they now begin to freeze. I attempt to brush it off, but the pain is incredible. My fingers are paralysed. I am unable to light the stove for almost 30 minutes as my fingers continue to throb with pain. Another good lesson re-learnt: just when you think you are safe and warm, you are not. Be diligent always!

We huddle in our bags while the storm settles in around us. Over a metre of snow is blown against the tents in the next 24 hours requiring constant removal; visibility is less than 20 metres, yet it is a rather mild −18°c. We have been on the ice for some time now,

and there are some very interesting and pungent aromas emanating from my nether regions. The aroma is so powerful that it offends even me! We have been working hard (with rivers of sweat running down my chest and back into my bum) with no opportunity to wash and no fresh underwear to change into. Large flakes of skin fall off my head. Red sores are appearing in my beard. I have substantial burst blisters on both heels. My shoulders ache continually. My coccyx is in constant sharp pain; it must have something to do with sleeping on ice every night. My left thigh is numb on the outer flank, not from cold but from awkward sleeping angles. It only returns to normal twelve months later. My body aches all over for the entire time that we are trekking in Antarctica. Antarctica is working me over. We collapse into our bags.

Chapter 9

IN THE TENT

The weather does not improve, so we settle in for some tent time. By now we are all very good at keeping warm and staying comfortable. Since I sleep alone in one tent with all the gear and food, I am able to enjoy the relative luxury of a private bathroom when the connecting annexe of the tents is zipped shut. This is most advantageous when the weather is particularly foul and I really need to go – and I am not talking about the pee bottle here! Pooing in a tent is a difficult, carefully thought through and diligently managed operation – you want to make sure that you get it right.

Step one.   Empty the contents of your bladder into your pee bottle before going any further. It is very important to remember this!

Step two.   Find a secure zip-lock bag with a very wide opening.

Step three.   Find a comfortable squatting position from which to 'direct traffic'.

Step four.   Clear the general area in case of unforeseen misadventure.

Step five.   Wait for things to happen naturally. This is not a situation that calls for any extra pressure to be exerted. 'Sure and steady' is the only approach.

Step six.   Carefully hold the bag wide open from the underside and be prepared to guide the motion in – utmost care is needed here.

Step seven.   Wipe and seal the bag and place it outside the tent to freeze before packing it onto the sledge for the return trip to Patriot Hills.

Step eight.   Wash hands thoroughly.

Bowel movements in the tent remind me of mountaineering story about two climbers who share a tent for several weeks, high on the mountain. They bond and get on very well together, sharing most things: they discuss their lives at home, their families' foibles and strengths. They even confess their darkest secrets. At the end of three weeks, one chap says to the other, 'Something is bothering me. There is something that I must ask you. Every day I struggle outside to do my daily business in the freezing wind and snow. I haven't seen you

go outside to do your business once! What is going on?' His friend responds, 'Every time you leave the tent to go outside, I do my business in a plastic bag and place it under your bed.'

I make several hot drinks for the Boss, Mertz and myself. All the popular flavoured drinks are now finished and we are drinking tea and hot chocolate. During the drinks preparation, some hot water will invariably spill on the tent floor; I simply leave it for a few minutes before picking it up as ice. At −45°C you can throw a cup of boiling water into the air and it will fall as snow. Outside the wind is relentless, constantly pushing snow over the tents. Every few hours, one of us gets up to clear snow from the tents. If it builds up too much, the flow of fresh air into the tent can be restricted, and there is also the possibility of the tents collapsing under the weight. We poke our heads out the vent at the top of the tent from time to time for a weather update: still snowing, visibility of less than 20 metres and wind roaring.

Photography: P. Hillary

The effects of wind on exposed skin at −20, −30 or −40°c need to be experienced to be believed. The slightest puff of breeze will lower the temperature instantly. When the wind is roaring, it can kill you if you are not adequately prepared. You must plan all movements carefully. The tying of a knot, the clipping of a buckle or the taking of a photograph becomes a dangerous task. You think to yourself, 'OK, I have 20 seconds to strap my crampons onto my boots before my fingers begin to freeze. What am I doing? What is the order of the steps that I must take? How long can I take? What are the risks? How quickly can I get my gloves back on?' If you muck up even a little, you will experience extreme pain and thawing out for half an hour or so; if you muck up a lot, you may lose your fingertips or worse. Today is a good day to stay in the tent.

We agree that there will be no travel, and we settle in for a day of conversation and storytelling. Mertz recounts the horror of the crevasse field of several days ago. He is very amusing – 'I just hate the bloody things!' We discuss what we are all doing together in this place, this other planet. I take out my writing pad and take notes.

After another round of hot drinks, we talk of fear and how it affects us. The Boss has experienced more fear than most and says, 'Fear is a good thing. It keeps you sharp and it keeps you thinking. Fear is part of the experience. You must accept it, absorb it – learn from it. You must let fear help you take responsibility for your own safety and ultimately your own destiny.' This partly explains how I felt on the frozen lip of the volcano in New Zealand and zigzagging through the crevasse field a few days ago. I hadn't stopped to think about it, but I had embraced my fear and made it a helpful tool rather than a burden.

The conversation moves on to the inevitable questions. Why are we here? What are we doing? Where are we going? For Mertz, 'It has to be the challenge of overcoming your fears and challenging yourself to achieve things that you never thought possible. Just being here is a dream for me. I mean, Boss, you have done a lifetime's worth of this kind of thing, and old Oates over there has had some great trips, some of them with me. We drove around Australia, crossing the Gibson Desert on the Gunbarrel Highway; we paddled down the Amazon in canoes for two weeks. It's all about getting out there and having a go. Not many friends of mine would even contemplate some of these activities. I mean most of my friends would curl up into a ball and cry themselves to death out here. But that's not the point. I love being in remote environments and it is an absolute treat to be here with great mates.'

I chime in, 'Well spoken, Mertz. It is a strange thing to find yourself in these places. I love the challenge too, and I also love knowing the quality of those who have come before us – not that I put myself in their class for a moment – but the knowledge that you have followed in their great footsteps in some small way. For me, the journey is what it is all about. It's what you find out about yourself that interests me. Being in different situations and challenging conditions helps me get to know myself better. It is so refreshing to get away from the easy Western lifestyle that we all lead. When I say "we all", I mean most of us Westerners have got it so easy that we wouldn't have a clue what it means to do it tough. We all have food, clothing and shelter. If we want water, we turn on a tap; we want light, we flick a switch; we want food, we go to the fridge; we want to be some place else; we jump in the car; we want anything and it is there for us in varying degrees, depending on our ability or willingness to spend. We want everything, but we know very little about life other than whatever it is that serves our own self-interest.'

'Interesting, Oates,' the Boss says. 'I think that you have summed it up with the journey aspect, which can get a bit hackneyed, but you and Mertz are spot on: it is all about getting out and "having a go". Why go on such journeys at all? I refer to this question in my book *In the Ghost Country*. I ask myself this question often.' He reads from his book:

> Part of the answer is that I'm drawn to the simplicity of the pilgrim's life, and the soaring emotions that go with it. As one Frank Smythe wrote in a little book called *The Mountain Top* given to me by my grandfather Jim Rose, who also climbed mountains, 'The charm of mountain-climbing lies not in the climbing, in success, nor in failure, but in the great range of emotions provoked through these physical experiences.'

> I think this observation was at the core of what lured Jim and my father and me to the mountains, and adventuring in general.

> Another part of the answer lies in the definition of what a challenge is all about. To me a challenge is an undertaking where, at the end of the day, the planned outcome is not assured. There is uncertainty. Hence, the Hillary formula: Challenge = Uncertainty = Excitement.

> No challenge worth its salt is going to be easy. I think there is merit in trying things that make you uncomfortable. Tackle the unknown, challenge yourself, and out of the abyss of the unknown rises the spectre of your own fear. To swing from the rudder of your own vessel and steer your ship through the weather of life, to chart a journey that you direct. You must do this. Because this is the only chance you will get.

The Boss looks up from the page. 'In many ways, you climb or go on great adventures because it stirs a passion within you. It is the same with anything.' Reading to us again:

> It is like falling in love. Different people are drawn to different men and women for many different and sometimes inexplicable reasons. That's how it is with pursuits that require passion and focus. The decision to climb and to keep on climbing is visceral and certainly intangible. In many ways, you climb because there is nothing else that you would rather do. And, like love, it is wild, it is difficult, it is marvellous, and it can hurt terribly.

'Thanks, Boss – very insightful,' says Mertz. 'Ah, Oates, can I have a nice big hot chocolate please? Boss, how about you?'

'Why not? With an extra spoon of milk please, Oates.'

'Coming up, gentlemen. I may be some time.'

When we have all settled back with a nice, big, rich hot chocolate with extra milk, I ask the Boss about his previous experience in Antarctica: 'We know it is cold – I mean, it's −30°c outside now – but how would you describe living in it for 72 days, as you did on your trek to the pole?'

It is remarkable to be sitting here, at 80 degrees south, with a man such as the Boss speaking to us so freely and generously of his life experiences. The Boss goes on to read us some more excerpts from his book, and he shares some thoughts on his life lived on the edge:

> The deep field cold soaks through everything, no matter how many socks and thermal suits you are wearing. It leaches out the warmth, freezes all moisture. Boots and bones are shattered, flesh freeze dried. A gentle gust of the deep sub zero burns the skin like acid. The cold eats you alive, quick or slow.

> Throw gallons of boiling water six feet into the air, at minus forty, and watch it turn to snow. Snap. Instant snow. Antarctica is called a desert because the deep sub zero keeps the air dry as dry. The dry cold air sucks on the throat and tongue and the lungs, draining out one's bodily moisture. Freeze dried, mummified ... The deep south of Antarctica is sterile. Nil life. That's the sort of cold it is ... On a long haul you are slowly running down. Wearing out.

'Boss, what can you tell us about your trip with Eric Philips and Jon Muir to the South Pole in 1998?' asks Mertz.

'It was bloody awful! For a start we never even had a training weekend together, and the sledges were too heavy. The damned things weighed 220 kilograms, that's 440 pounds. On the first day, I got to a little hummock, just a suggestion of a mound, and there was no way that I was going to get over it. Hauling and hauling – nothing but horror. Philips had this obsession about numbers and dates and how far we had come and how much distance we had to make up. I tried to explain that despite having put too much weight in our sledges, we just needed to work into our task, that we would improve as time went on and that he should just relax a little and enjoy the trip. I think that just got him angrier. He was critical of how I was moving when it seemed not to be a problem. The food he organised was appalling – awful to eat – I mean it had all the fats and energy, but it was nearly inedible. Very different from your fine catering here, Oates, I must say!'

'Thank you, Boss. More hot chocolate?'

'Lovely! Yes, every breakfast was swimming in oil, lard, fat or all three. Look, it was poorly planned, poorly conceived and one big controversy really. I mean Philips gave me a fearful and rather unnecessary blast on *60 Minutes*, if you recall. In the end it was just all about him and his tantrum really. In the book I describe it as the loneliest trip of my life.'

> I know that the burning emptiness sucked on my mind and my emotions. Just pulled them out like cotton stuffing. That's the kind of place it is. I know that the atmosphere in that tent with my companions became stranger and stranger, until it became nasty, alienating. We needed to be mates, like the Old Firm, and look after one another to get through that place in reasonable shape. But there is no happy photo of the three of us on my study wall.

'Geez, Boss. How bad did it get?' asks Mertz.

Fish eye lens

Photographer: P. Hillary

'Well, I didn't think I could rely on my companions. I didn't feel particularly safe with them – I was already talking to the dead. Hallucinating. My dead friends who came to me on the ice were the only company I had.'

Fred, on Everest. Tripped and fell. I was there at the time.

Craig. Everest. Tripped and fell. There at the time.

Ken. Ama Dablam. Terrible head wound, most likely dead when we cut the rope.

Jeff. K2. In his sleeping bag. Yes, there too.

Bill. Makalu. Swept off and buried. We had to keep sounding upbeat in case he could hear us talking as we were poking the rubble for him.

Mark. Makalu. Tripped and fell. That's what the tracks said, yes.

Mike. Everest, a few years after one of our own attempts. Fell asleep while sitting down up high. Didn't wake up.

Rob. Everest. We climbed it together, for the first time together, five years before he died near the South Summit. Most famous for calling his pregnant wife from where he lay down. He told her not to worry too much.

Gary. Dead three years after we climbed Everest together with Rob. Dhaulagiri.

My mother.

My sister.

The Captain [Scott] …

By the time these things came to mind, the dead friends on the march, tension in the tent, I had already started carrying the stove and the bivvy sack, making sure I always had them in my sled. I wasn't going to be left for dead. And that's how things were on our trip, after about two weeks out.

When I talked to Dad about some of these … issues, he said, 'Well, that's the way it goes sometimes.'

'Bloody hell, Boss! You had little bit on!' says Mertz, the king of understatement.

'Yes, I did, and it was bloody awful.'

Kelley Peak

Chapter 10

WHITEOUT

We are so thoroughly snowed in at camp three that it takes us more than four hours to dig out the tents, pack up the camp and load it onto our sledges. The sledges are now being towed backwards, which will add significantly to the drag. We look around for any gear left behind before hauling away. Today we make a short trek of around 10 kilometres before relenting to the katabatic and establishing camp four. We go to sleep that night hoping for improved conditions tomorrow.

The next morning however, the conditions are ordinary at best, with visibility no better that 20 metres; the spindrift blows furiously on the fierce katabatic at 35 knots; snow is still falling, and the temperature is a cool –30°c. We decide that we will try to make the 32 kilometres to Patriot Hills camp today as we have received a report that the weather is clearing to the north and tomorrow may be a flying day. If it is, we don't want to miss it, as we know only too well how difficult it can be to get the Ilyushin onto the blue ice runway at Patriot Hills. If we miss the flight, we could be here for another three weeks. Did I mention that it is now late December and I am expected home for Christmas?

The Boss takes the lead and hauls into the wind, with Mertz and me following closely behind. Visibility is down to 10 metres at times; we are moving in what is known as a total whiteout. There is no horizon, no sun, no sky, no ground – only white. There are no visual markers of any description. The roar of the wind is so strong that the only way to communicate is to shout at them from close range, physically grab them or prod them with my ski pole.

The weather deteriorates further. The wind swings around to a headwind and has increased to 40 knots, gusting at up to 60 knots. Visibility has not improved. These conditions have to be experienced to be believed, it's as though I am fighting my way through cappuccino froth. The compass is our lifeline; our course is 93 degrees. We always seem to be going uphill. My instinct is to turn away from the wind, but this would be a mistake as it would send me off course. Spindrift blasts into me like lead fired from a shotgun. I feel like I am trapped in a small room, such is the claustrophobic nature of a whiteout. Everything seems to be pressing in on me. It is incredible how much we depend on visual markers to find our way.

Making it through the whiteout is simply a matter of placing one ski ahead of the other, then the other, then the other, then the other. The compass bearing is locked on 93 degrees. I glance down at it from time to time and am impressed that the Boss is never off course. I keep double-checking though, as I am loath to leave the navigating to one person. I follow the Boss closely. Each step of his ski is mirrored by mine. I mimic his every movement. He quickens, I quicken. He drifts east, I drift east. To stop and adjust equipment or have a drink will mean losing the Boss within a few seconds into the whiteout with little prospect of finding him. I follow very closely. Every part of me is covered up. I wear a mask and hat under my jacket hood, but the wind roars right through me. It is very cold now, with the wind blasting the icy spindrift into my face. I have no idea how far we have travelled; I don't

Researchers camp under cloud

wear a watch, so there are no clues as to how long we have been going. All I know is that I am doing it pretty tough; the others guys must be feeling it too by now.

The wind has carved out deep sculptural channels in the snow and ice known as sastrugi which make travel more difficult. Up and down, over and across, up and down, over and across. The sledges, being towed backwards, don't glide easily over this terrain. They are frequently catching on the edges and lip of the sastrugi. It is a struggle to keep my extremities warm. My toes are constantly wriggled in my boots between steps. I twitch my fingers around in my mittens in an attempt to generate some warmth. In short, it is cold, windy, white and particularly unpleasant!

There is no communication or contact between the team members. We each have no idea how the others are going. I do know the Boss is doing a brilliant job up front, but I can't imagine how tough it is to lead in these conditions. My time will come. The Boss comes to a halt, and I notice that he is a little unstable on his feet. As we cover the last few metres to reach him, he overbalances and falls to the ground. Bloody hell! Now Mertz arrives. We have been hauling for more than four hours. The Boss is feeling a little bit off, so we decide that this will be the place for our lunch break.

We grab our down jackets and lunch from the top of our packs. I check that everyone has their thermoses and a pack to sit on before we attempt the descent into the bivvy bag. The wind threatens to rip the bivvy bag from our hands. We all stand face to face as we slip the bivvy bag down as far as it will go before slowly bending our knees until our bums land on the backpacks. After much wriggling, grunting and shuffling about, the tiny covering is secure and we are all seated. With the wind shut out, the bivvy bag slowly warms up. Our spirits are lifted by simply being out of the wind and spindrift. Gloves are removed and lunch is served.

The Boss attempts to confirm our position with the GPS as I make hot soups for the team. The Boss reports that we are rather dramatically off course. My heart sinks. I look across at him and I feel better, not because he looks well but because I am in better shape than him at this stage and will be able to assist him. He is in a slight daze and feeling a bit off colour after his exceptional effort over the past four hours. Mertz and I nod knowingly at each other. It turns out the Boss has made a programming error with the GPS and we are not lost after all. He just needs plenty of hot drinks and some warming up. Make no mistake, we have just completed a gruelling four-hour non-stop haul through a whiteout into the teeth of a gale and are desperate to rest and refuel. Drinking the warm fluids is very restorative.

We are all sipping at our hot soup drinks now, and after a few minutes I see the Boss's colour and vitality return. Seeing him in that vulnerable condition has certainly given both Mertz and me a jolt. We decide that Mertz and I will take the lead for the remainder of the haul to Patriot Hills, calculating that we are almost halfway there. We have covered 10 kilometres in

Whiteout

four hours of travel, with another 11 kilometres to go. We have still got plenty on! As we sip our hot soups, we feel our energy levels lift immediately. Hands are now warm, and toes are moving, cooperating again. I offer a second round of hot drinks, this time with some melon flavouring. Mertz quips, 'It is like putting oil into a burnt-out old motor.'

We take an hour-long break to rehydrate and to get ourselves organised. By the time we are ready to pack up and set off again, the mood in the tiny windswept bivvy sack is positively upbeat. Another four hours hauling into this wretched gale and we will be back at Patriot Hills camp. It has turned so cold now that I dare not remove my down jacket. This is a first for the trip. I am so snug and warm. Up goes the bivvy bag as the freezing air grabs hold of us again. We decide that I will take the lead. I check my compass – 93 degrees. I diligently check my sledge – all is secured – and then I check my backpack – all is as it should be. I check with Mertz and the Boss, and they are prepared for departure. Off we go.

The whiteout continues, I have run out of adjectives to describe the conditions we endure, the spindrift hits us as if propelled by a sandblasting machine. I have the compass in my right hand as I plod along. It is impossible to watch the compass and hold my line into the wind. I look at the compass, take the bearing of 93 degrees and haul straight ahead for 10 or 20 metres before checking the compass again. I am off course immediately. I have never navigated in such adversity before and I am yet to learn the correct way to do it. I plod on. Again I drift off course within a few minutes. My respect for the Boss and for what he has achieved earlier in the day soars. This leading in the whiteout is a very difficult business.

The Boss is behind, screaming that we are going way off course. Of course I realise this but am powerless to hold a dead straight course. We stop to reassess. I explain how difficult I am finding it to follow the compass and ski at the same time. Offering no advice as to how it should be done, the Boss determinedly takes the lead again. I still cannot work out the secret of getting on course and staying there for any period of time. The Boss leads on.

After a while – in the interests of saving the Boss's energy and skills in case we should need them later – we agree to give Mertz a crack at leading us through the blizzard. Mertz dusts the spindrift off his compass and takes up poll position. After quickly setting his bearings, and in vintage Mertz fashion, he dashes off into the white without consulting his compass for more than two minutes. He is clearly drifting to the east. The Boss yells out for Mertz to stop. I look down at my compass to see that Mertz has drifted 100 degrees off course in the two minutes he has been leading. Jeepers! This leading business is proving most difficult. It has just clicked for me what needs to be done to hold a straight course.

'Mertz, you are 100 degrees off course!' the Boss yells.

'That's impossible – I can't be! I just looked at the compass and 93 degrees is over there.'

He points towards 93 degrees, which is not the way that he is leading us. The Boss wants to lead again, but given what happened earlier in the day I want him to be fresh for later on in case he is required for any major dramas. At one point Mertz claims his compass isn't working! There is palpable tension in the air – not good.

'Boss, Mertz, I will lead now. Boss, I have worked out what needs to be done. You cannot take your eyes off the compass for even a second or you drift off course. I now fully understand this. Let's go!'

I haul ahead but it's not easy. My right hand, holding the compass, is held up in front of my face. Both ski poles are in my left hand. It's hard to get any rhythm going with only my left arm available to swing and push. I try some variations on this position, but none works very well. I will just have to tough it out. I cannot believe that the Boss did this non-stop for four hours. I am feeling the pinch after half an hour. I get a glimpse of what the explorers from the Heroic Age must have endured: the monotony and the cold, miserable feeling that you must continue with this wretched hauling for months on end. There are no guarantees that you will survive the ordeal. The man whose name I have taken lodges in my head.

What was Oates feeling as he plodded back from the pole? I understand that his pain must have been considerable and that his apparent dislike of Scott must have gnawed at him. I wonder what thoughts passed through his mind. He knew that he was going to die. He knew that he would never see his loved ones again. He gave his life so that the others would have a chance to save their own. Oates' last recorded words – 'I am just going outside and may be some time' – stick with me. They have been a part of my life since the day I first read them 25 years ago. I wonder what Oates would have been like to talk to. I reckon that he would have been a great bloke with whom to have a beer and a yarn. I imagine drinking with him in a smoky pub with a low roof. My mind wanders.

I haul ahead. Hauling, hauling, never lifting my eyes from the compass – 93 degrees. The spindrift builds up on the compass housing that covers the magnetic needle. I brush it off. I drift off into various day dreams. Sometimes I am lazing in my warm bed at home with Caroline. Sometimes I am lying on a sunny beach. I am always resting, always warm. For a time my concentration turns to the wind that is blasting spindrift into my face from almost directly ahead. I say '*almost* directly ahead' as the direction of the wind is slightly off centre, coming from one o'clock (if twelve o'clock is directly ahead). I stare down at the compass. I look up again. My natural instinct is to turn away from the wind. My 93 degree bearing points me into the wind. I have no option but to push on – straight ahead. My shoulders ache; my legs are becoming heavy, and it seems like an eternity since I took over the lead. My sledge is particularly sluggish. My right arm, that has been holding the compass in front of my face, is about to fall off. How long have we been going?

I feel a thump on my shoulder. It is Mertz, bless him. I have been leading for more than two hours. It is three hours since the lunch break. Mertz is ready for a burst in the lead. I remind him that he cannot take his eyes off the compass for even a second. There will be no dashing out the front this time. The Boss does some quick calculations, which place us within a few kilometres of Patriot Hills camp. Mertz stays the line and does a remarkable job of leading us for what we hope will be the last leg of our whiteout haul. The visibility has improved somewhat and we can now see for almost 50 metres at times. Mertz has picked the speed up and we are hiking along, although it all still seems to be uphill with no end in sight.

We push on and on. After an hour, Mertz yells out, but I am unable to hear him over the roaring wind. The Boss and I move up to Mertz's shoulder. Not only has he led us brilliantly to the Promised Land, but he has also, incredibly, spotted the tail fins of the Twin Otter aircraft off to the right. Absolute genius! Well done, Mertz! We all embrace and cheer like schoolboys. After ten of the most inhuman hours we are likely ever to experience, we have finally made it back. We are ecstatic. The last 100 metres are covered quickly and with great enthusiasm. I arrive at the door of the mess tent, and without pausing, I burst inside – skis and all – before dropping my pack to the ground and pulling the remains of my sledge in with me. The others follow quickly.

Euphoria overcomes us as we hug each other and cheer. It is thirteen hours since the day began with the packing up of camp four. The hot water is boiling. The fuel stove is roaring. The floor is dry and solid. I can stand upright without crouching. I can sit in a real chair. I can take off the frozen layers of gear and feel warm. We all cheer and hug again. It feels like we have walked into a five-star hotel. We are absolutely delighted and congratulate each other on our efforts. Desperately thirsty and dry, I rummage through the supplies in the mess tent. I sit down and consume 2 litres of delicious, sweet strawberry jelly before my thirst is quenched. My boots are off and my feet are propped up on a chair in front of the fuel heater. The luxury of this moment is not lost on me as I sit back to appreciate and contemplate the most simple pleasures in life – food, drink, warmth and shelter.

Our debrief begins an hour later, when we have all settled down a little. We conclude that none of us had much left in the main tank and that, had we not made it back when we did, the reserve tank would have been required within the hour. We are overjoyed at reaching the warmth of the mess tent and decide that we will not put the tents up tonight but will sleep in the mess tent. You beauty!

Then, just when we think that things cannot get any better, a tall, bearded gentleman of Nordic appearance enters the mess tent. He introduces himself to the Boss: 'Hello, my name is Børge Ousland.' The Boss is taken aback at meeting his hero so unexpectedly, and as he reaches to take Børge's outstretched hand, he only just manages to say, 'Peter … Peter Hillary.' We all settle down for a chat with our new best friend, Børge Ousland, the world's greatest polar adventurer. Oh, the people you meet!

Chapter 11

BACK AT PATRIOT HILLS

We are utterly exhausted after the ordeal of our 13 hour day and enjoy a deep 12 hour sleep. Over the next few days, we spend time with Børge and his travelling companions, Fredrik and Jan Eric from Norway. Having just completed the last degree to the South Pole, they have been waiting patiently for the weather to clear for a week now. (Completing the last degree involves being flown to 89 degrees south and being left to trek the last degree to the South Pole.) Apart from the camp crew – approximately fifteen ALE employees, who are here for the three-month season – we are the only people in camp.

Fredrick shows me to an intricate 1000-piece jigsaw puzzle of a massive tulip field, which he has recently started. I immediately set to work on it. I have not done a jigsaw puzzle since I was twelve and love the challenge it presents. It's also refreshing to get the brain working on something other than staying warm and moving forwards.

Polar plateau

After a rest day we have recovered sufficiently for our next mission – a day-trip traverse and climb of the Patriot Hills. Skis are left behind, and we travel light for this climb, with only one pack between the three of us. The weather is fair, but thankfully not too windy as we set off towards the runway, which is being furiously cleared of snow by the two snow-blowing machines. The climb is rather steep to begin with, taking us across a scree of rocks before levelling out on a rocky plateau. It is quite strange to be walking on rocks again after spending the past two weeks on snow and ice. The rock here has been exposed by the constant howling of the katabatic wind, which strips away any snow that tries to settle.

As we near the summit, the wind picks up significantly. We round the summit ridge and are very nearly blown off the mountain. We crawl the last 20 metres so that we don't get blasted away. The Boss is very keen to stand on the summit, while Mertz and I are somewhat less ambitious, preferring to keep at least three points of contact with the mountain at all times. We stand briefly for some quick photographs. The views across Marble Hills and Independence Hills to the polar plateau are breathtaking, and so is the wind that has increased to gusts of 50 knots. We pause for a few quick snaps and then get the hell out of there as fast as we can.

Patriot Hills ridge and Horseshoe Valley

Fredrik's puzzle

Patriot Hills summit approach

Patriot Hills and views from the climb

Patriot Hills camp

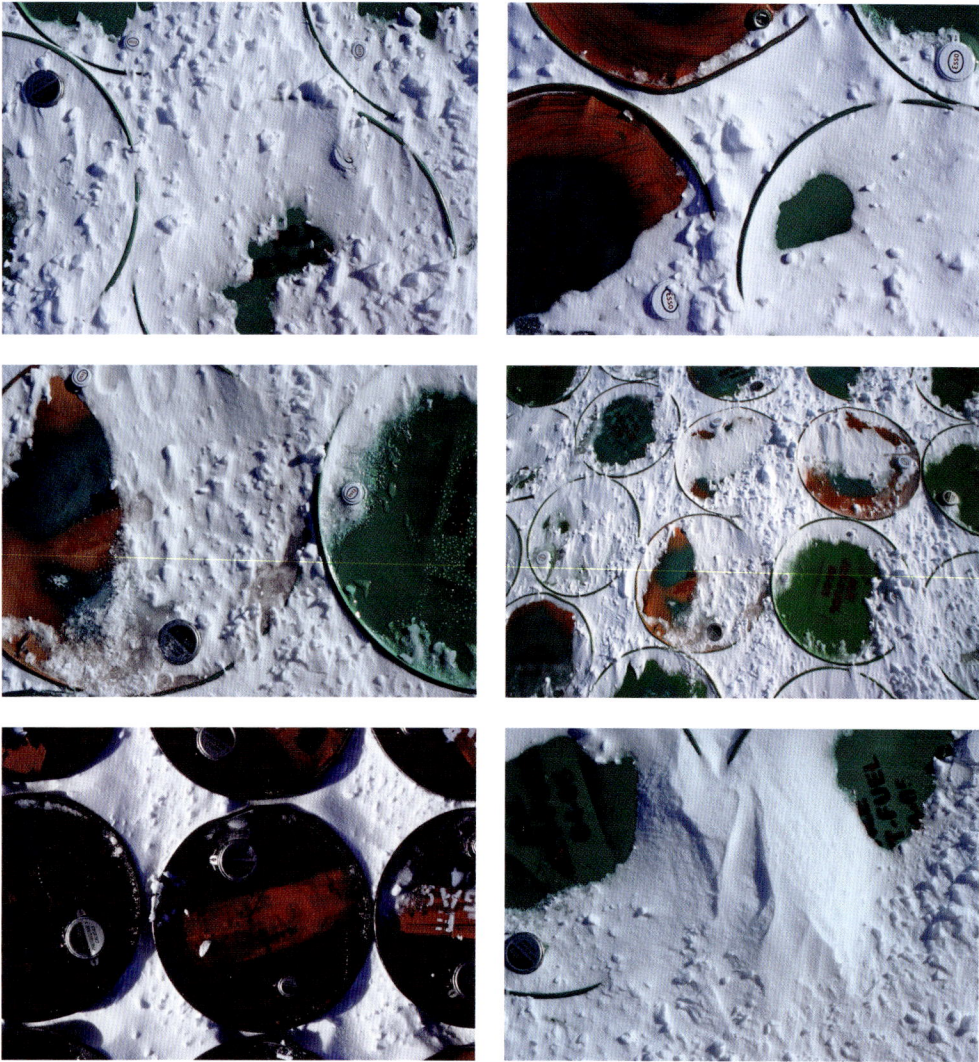

Fuel barrels

When we reach the base of the Patriot Hills, I take some time to wander around and photograph the ice, snow and rocks. It is a real thrill to be able to take the time to indulge myself like this. I wander onto the runway for a closer look. Then I walk over to the fuel barrels that have been emptied and are waiting to be returned to Punta on the Ilyushin. They are jammed side by side and partially covered by snow, looking like six packs of beer on ice. They make wonderful photographic subjects and remind me of an earlier series that I photographed in Australia entitled *Dead Cars and Rusty Barrels*. Again I am finding similarities and odd juxtapositions between the deserts of Australia and the frozen plateaus of Antarctica – silent, clean, unpopulated, remote and wild. The stacked fuel drums are a further reminder of man's temporary and tentative grip on the land.

Next we take a look at some tracks that we made while out walking yesterday in the fresh snow. The wind has since stripped away the surrounding snow, leaving only the compressed snow from our footprints, which now sit 5 centimetres above ground level. These raised footprints are a remarkable Antarctic quirk.

The Boss needs the Ilyushin to fly out in the next day or two if he is to make it home to New Zealand for a few days with his family before Christmas. Just after Christmas he is booked to lecture on a cruise ship in – wait for it – the Antarctic Peninsula! If he cannot get back home, he will have to go directly to Santiago, Chile, to board the ship on its journey south. On the bright side, one of his daughters will be joining him on the ship. Did I mention that the Boss is a very busy man?

We receive news of the British party and their converted Ford – the *Global Challenger*. They arrived at the South Pole after only 69 hours, setting a world record for travel to the pole by vehicle. We hope to catch up with them all in the next few days. Across at Mount Vinson, conditions have improved somewhat, with most groups successfully reaching the summit. This improvement in the weather only came after all groups were pinned down by high winds and storm activity, forcing them to spend more than a week in their tents waiting, waiting, waiting!

The weather has cleared, the wind has dropped and the skies are clear – perfect conditions for flying. There is one small problem though: the runway is still covered with snow from the recent falls, and it will take two days to clear. The Norwegians are not happy about having to wait for another two days, and they let the camp manager know all about it when she gives us the weather update. Børge is the most vocal: 'We have snow in Norway too you know. Just get it off!' Once the news of the further delay has been digested and accepted, we get chatting to Børge about his next adventure.

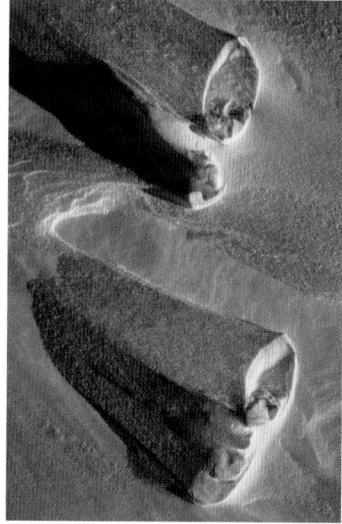

Raised footprints

Blue ice runway

He tells us that his next undertaking will be to ski, swim and haul across the Arctic to the North Pole. Børge casually adds that he and his travelling companion, Mike Horn, will depart on 23 January and that the trek should take approximately sixty 60 days. We are speechless! Børge will set out on this adventure in the depths of winter, in total darkness and with temperatures hovering around –45°c. His plans are barely credible.

Suffice to say, no person has ever attempted this before. There is no landmass at the North Pole; it is covered with drifting ice sheets. Børge has designed a waterproof, floating sledge, which is important, as Børge plans to jump in and swim when confronted with open water. Yes, that's right: jump in and swim! I believe that backstroke is his stroke of choice. It will be dark and very, very cold. Børge will be wearing a headlamp and carrying a .44 Magnum revolver to deal with any disagreeable polar bears he may encounter. This guy is a serious athlete – the world's pre-eminent polar traveller. Think of Lance Armstrong, Roger Federer and Tiger Woods rolled into one elite endurance performer.

Meeting Børge Ousland is a thrill for us all. Here we are just hanging out, playing cards, making cups of tea for each other, doing the puzzle, and chatting about life and its challenges, in these remote parts. Børge is an approachable and level-headed guy who just wants to get home to see his family like the rest of us. Having heard all the stories about Børge's feats of endurance from the Boss, I am overcome with an overwhelming desire just to touch him so that I can feel what an athlete of his calibre feels like. I have shaken hands with him, but I just want to get and idea of how strong he feels. Short of challenging him to a fight, I wonder how I can manage this. Someone suggests a photograph of us all. Perfect! I jump in next to Børge, and we put our arms firmly around each other's shoulders. He feels like steel, a rock! I am not disappointed. It is impossible to tell where the muscle stops and the shoulder blade starts. On returning home we follow Børge's progress on his website (www.ousland.com) as he successfully completes his two-month trek to the North Pole.

Mess tent

The next five days are spent waiting for weather updates, preparing meals, going for long walks, going for a ski, taking photographs, doing the puzzle, reading and general camp gossip. I enjoy waiting here, unlike our time in Punta. I am in the middle of a pristine wilderness enjoying day trips to Patriot Hills (the hills not the camp). There are countless hours of wandering around Patriot Hills exploring with my camera and the fascinating company of the world's leading mountaineers and polar travellers.

We receive news that three of the British *Global Challenger* crew are flying back from the pole in a Twin Otter and will be landing in a few hours. We decide to go for a walk and wait for them. We are at the runway to greet Andrew, Andrew and Richard, who took advantage of the flight back to get a different perspective, to say nothing of avoiding the very long and rough trip back from the pole. It is great to see them all so pumped up and pleased with their drive down to the pole and with the time they spent there camping out and waiting for a flight back to Patriot Hills. The camp crew invite us in for a celebratory dinner. It is 2 a.m. – brilliant sunshine.

Rock samples awaiting collection

Twin Otter

The Brits tell us all about their rugged drive down on the *Global Challenger* and how they nearly drove into a crevasse.

The *Global Challenger* had performed extremely well, and Gunnie had driven superbly through the huge sastrugi fields they encountered. There was some dissention, however, in the *Global Challenger* camp when the lads announced that they wanted to fly back to Patriot Hills. It seems that Gunnie (now a national hero in his home of Iceland) was furious when told of this change of plan. Anyway, they sorted it all out, and Gunnie is now driving back with team leader Jason and filmmaker Andrew. He is under strict instructions not to beat the 69-hour record set earlier by the *Challenger*. Naturally Gunnie ignores this instruction and makes the return trip in less than two days, following his original tracks and setting another record!

There is tension brewing at Patriot Hills as the leaders of the camp crew seem more interested in their own timetables than in doing everything possible to get us all home for Christmas. For some reason, unbeknown to us, the camp leader is unwilling to give us all the information relating to a possible flight. She wants to keep it to herself and release it selectively, but her crew is leaking information to us like a sieve. A few standoffs ensue, and some strong words are used by the most outspoken and frustrated members of the trekking and climbing teams. This results in more open and honest communication and eventually both groups seem to settle down.

Fastest to the Pole – the *Global Challenger* crew

Chapter 12

LAST NIGHT ON THE FROZEN CONTINENT

As we have been back in Patriot Hills camp for more than five days, ALE rules allow us to tap into the mysterious underground cache that has been dug into the snow and ice. This holds the food supply for the entire camp for the three-month summer season. It is a huge manmade underground freezer. Here we are given two cans of frozen mussels and a packet of pasta for this evening's meal. The cache is an underground maze of tunnels, chambers and food-filled boxes. A chainsaw is used whenever they need to make more space for storage or to create a new tunnel to connect two chambers.

After what can only be described as an interesting dinner of frozen mussel pasta in the mess tent, Mertz and I wander over to the communications tent for an update on the chances of flying out in the next 24 hours. After discussions with the Patriot Hills logistics crew, the radio call comes through from Punta Arenas. I am asked to leave the communications tent. During this call I can sense the desperation in the voice of the radio operator back in Punta as he checks and re-checks the weather outlook with Jaco (pronounced 'Yako'). Jaco has spent the past three Antarctic summers at Patriot Hills as the resident weatherman, calling the weather on all the flights. His knowledge of the weather patterns is impressive, despite having spent just three seasons in Antarctica with very limited resources. The radio operator in Punta makes a phone call to the Russian crew and the pressure begins to mount.

Everyone is desperate to get out. Christmas is fast approaching and we all have commitments at home. The radio crackles to life again. The Russian crew want more stable weather patterns. Further discussion takes place. More and more people are gathering around the communications tent for the latest news. I signal to them to be quiet and to stay away if they cannot be quiet. At this point the logistics boss, distracted by the rising commotion outside, storms out of the communications tent and tells us all to piss off. We slowly shuffle off like a bunch of naughty school children.

Ten minutes later the communications tent empties and we are given the news that there is no flight tonight, but Jaco will be up at 5 a.m. to see if we have a fly day. Conditions seem perfect, and there are further rumblings in the camp about the decision not to fly now.

The cache entrance

Laundry day

I feel like some fresh air and would welcome an opportunity to get away for a few hours from the tension that is brewing, so I discuss the possibility of a late-night ski with the Boss and Mertz. The Boss decides against it. Mertz and I prepare the gear for our trek. We only take a light pack between us loaded with thermos, cameras and film. It is as if the weather has returned from our arrival day: the sky is a brilliantly clear, bright blue and the air is almost still, which is incredible given the brutal conditions of the past weeks. Skiing without backpack or sledge is very liberating: the skis slide out easily from under my feet without having to heave forward with every step. It is 10 p.m. It looks like a fly day.

We ski out from camp in a north-easterly direction along the Twin Otter runway, before linking up with the Hercules runway and following it to the end. I am gliding along with Mertz by my side. The wind has dropped, and the air is perfectly still for the first time in more than two weeks. The sun is shining brightly. I am confident of a fly day tomorrow. I speak with Caroline on the satellite phone and tell her that I love her. I am the happiest man in the world. By the time we reach the end of the Hercules runway, it is past midnight. The low light is perfect for photography, and I shoot roll after roll trying to capture the magnificence of this place. Although I have progressed to the digital camera, this camera was left at home after reading its manual which does not reccommend use at or below freezing.

Mertz is keen to find the elusive DC-6 airplane that is reported to have crash-landed out this way somewhere. It went down years ago when its pilot had to make a forced landing in a whiteout. He managed to save the passengers. We are told that the tail is the only visible section. We are given GPS coordinates to locate the aircraft, but we choose instead to go by sight. The land is almost featureless, so a 2-metre DC-6 tail should be easy to spot, given the clear conditions and abundant sunlight …

When we glimpse an irregularity on the horizon, we guess it must be the tail of the DC-6 and ski towards it. As we draw closer, our suspicions are confirmed. I don't want to go on about it, but I will anyway. My gloves are off, I wear a light jacket, my down jacket is packed in case of any sudden weather changes. I stop skiing and talk with Mertz about the wonder of this environment – the great white everywhere. There is no sign of any life other than ours. You might as well be on Jupiter's frozen moon, Europa. We both agree that this evening is one of the highlights of our lives.

When we reach the DC-6, we have a scratch around and take some photographs before turning for home. It is almost 3 a.m. now, and we have been out for five hours having the time of our lives. The skis move so easily underfoot without the loads we have been carrying; it is as though we are walking on air. Our mood is very buoyant as we are almost certain that we will be flying tomorrow. In fact, the Ilyushin should be called right now. But the camp crew are asleep, so that's not going to happen. It is now 4 a.m.; Jaco will be up in an hour.

We ski back into camp at 5 a.m., and head straight for the mess tent and a big bowl of cereal and milk. We have just enjoyed possibly the best seven hours on skis of our lives. We do a quick calculation with the GPS and the map to find that we have just skied more than 25 kilometres. Mertz and I give each other a big hug of congratulations and celebration before collapsing into the tent at 6 a.m. This last ski means that we have travelled a little over 200 kilometres during our time in Antarctica. Surely we will fly tomorrow.

The Boss, Mertz and Oates

Oates, Børge and Mertz

Fredrik and Børge

We are woken by a general buzz of activity in the camp. It is 10 a.m. Through a vent in the tent, I yell out to a passer-by, 'Are we flying today?'

'Yes, the Ilyushin has been called. It departed Punta two hours ago and will be here at midday!'

'You little beauty!' We are out of here.

The tents are quickly packed, as is all the other equipment and gear. There is time for a final katabatic hoosh, which we all enjoy in the glorious sunshine with the Norwegians. What a fine hoosh! We leave some unused supplies in the mess tent.

The Ilyushin loading for departure

We load our equipment onto the huge motorised sledge before walking down to the blue ice runway. The Ilyushin makes a perfect landing at twelve noon, to the cheers of the waiting crowd. The Ilyushin unloads its cargo of people and hardware before we board and take our seats. The plane is then reloaded with all our gear, spent fuel drums, machinery for repair and finally rubbish. As this is taking place, we watch the weather deteriorate rapidly, to the point where the wind is blowing at more than 25 knots. Suddenly these are not flying conditions. This will be very interesting!

As the wind blows up, the pilot comes sprinting through the Ilyushin screaming, 'Up! Up! Up!' He grabs the last of the rubbish being loaded and drop kicks it off the ramp and onto the blue ice. He is now shouting at his cabin crew to close the hatch and to get everyone buckled in before take-off. Now! He dashes back to the cockpit, hurdling over bags, fuel drums and cargo nets.

The engines roar to life, and we are off. It is 4 p.m. Mertz and I agree that while the flyover looked spectacular from the ground when the Ilyushin arrived, we have no desire for the pilot to be showing off now that we are onboard. Just get us out of here – now! The jets roar and we hurtle down the blue ice. Lift off! But there is surprisingly little power. No – this feels terrible. What's happening? I sit rigid with fear for what seems an eternity while the Ilyushin, barely idling, swoops around to the right to complete the low flyover of Patriot Hills camp. Finally the pilot opens her up and lets more fuel into the engine. We lift up and up and my fears ease with every foot climbed.

The return flight is only four hours and is uneventful. I sleep most of the way on top of the baggage in the middle of the aircraft. We clear customs in Punta and load everything onto the bus that will deliver us to our hotel and our first shower in almost three weeks. Everyone on the bus stinks so badly that I barely notice the horrific smells emanating yet again from my underwear. Nasty, really nasty! On arrival at the hotel, we dash to the desk, check in, get our key and get to the room.

The hot shower and soap are the most delightful combination I can imagine. The longest time I have been without a shower was a month spent kayaking on Prince William Sound, Alaska. This shower seems better somehow, medicinal almost, probably because it is fresher in the mind. How good it is. It is only when I get out, all lovely and clean, that I begin to notice the smell of my trekking gear. When I open the bathroom door and get a nostril-full of Mertz, the Boss and my own recently discarded underwear, I am overwhelmed by the stench.

I open the windows to air out the hotel room. Before long we find ourselves at the Hotel Noriega with beers and cigars. Neither ever tasted so good. Unfortunately it is Sunday, and most places are closed or closing, but I suspect that in the morning we will realise that this is a good thing. As I slip into bed I cannot help but delight in the luxury of the crisp, clean sheets on my clean, naked skin. I sleep soundly.

Our only task before departure is to confirm our flights and get the tickets reissued before 11 a.m. at the Lan Chile office around the corner. We pack our bags and arrive at 10 a.m, only to find the office jam-packed with more than a hundred people, so we decide to take a ticket and come back later. We get ticket number 57. They are up to ticket number 20. There is plenty of time for breakfast at Lomits, the wonderful local nosh house with the rhyming name ...

Breakfast completed, we return to the Lan Chile office at 10.45 a.m., fifteen minutes before the cut-off time for reissue. Ticket number 45 is called. I turn to Mertz and ask if he has his passport and ticket. He responds in the affirmative. At 10.55 a.m. our ticket number is called and I present my ticket and passport, as does the Boss. The kind lady at the counter asks Mertz for his ticket and passport. He begins to fumble hurriedly through his papers. After some uncontrolled giggling from the Boss and myself, Mertz finally declares the ticket missing. We are in shock. I respond in a knee-jerk way. I cannot help but look aghast at Mertz and exclaim, 'You bloody idiot!' The English-speakers in the office turn to witness the unfolding commotion.

Mertz fumbles around unsuccessfully for an explanation. The Boss and I are laughing now as Mertz asks what he should do. We shout in stereo, '*Run!*' and with that, Mertz bursts from the Lan Chile office and runs directly into a well-built young man in the street, who is sent flying headlong into the gutter. Mertz just keeps on running and disappears into the crowded streetscape. It is now 11 a.m. and I must stall the lady who is reissuing our tickets until Mertz returns so that he is not forced to wait in line for another hour and miss the flight. My ticket is done and the Boss hands over his paperwork.

The lady at the counter is almost finished reissuing the Boss's ticket when Mertz blasts through the door (no casualties this time) waving his ticket and passport before collapsing into the seat at the desk. What a entertaining man. He is now in a lather of sweat, and the unwanted sprint to the hotel and back has brought on a horrific bout of reflux. He is heaving raucously. With our tickets all confirmed, we leave the Lan Chile office for a full debrief on the dash for the documents. We find a quiet place in the town square.

'I am sorry, team,' Mertz begins, 'I just don't know what happened then. I thought that I had the bloody tickets, but obviously I did not.'

I try to speak through my laughter. 'Mertz, I could not help but notice that you knocked a man to the ground as you burst out of the Lan Chile office. Do you have anything further to add?'

'No, Oates, nothing! Except that he was in no hurry to get up.'

I look over to a park bench and point at it before asking, 'Did you hurdle that park bench?'

'Yes.'

Sastrugi in the foreground with Ellsworth Mountains in the distance

'Any problems at the hotel?'

'You wouldn't bloody believe it, the room key didn't work, so I had to grab the maid, who was in the hallway at the time, and ask her to open the door for me. She looked at me a little suspiciously but sensed my seething desperation and opened it immediately. Oh my God, I need a seat and a glass of water.'

I give Mertz my bottle of water and he guzzles.

That afternoon we gather our baggage and load it onto the bus for the airport. The bus drives past the spot where Shackleton came ashore, past the old whaling station and finally past the Chilean Air Force base. The flight home is, thankfully, uneventful. On arrival, the first thing that strikes me is the warm air – warm enough to walk without shoes. In the past 48 hours we have gone from $-30°c$ to $35°c$, a 65-degree temperature shift.

Another thing that strikes me – perhaps even more than the warm air – is how easy life is away from the frozen plateaus of Antarctica. I recall Shackleton's observation that, 'No person who has not spent a period of his life in those stark and sullen solitudes that sentinel the Pole will understand fully what trees and flowers, sun-flecked turf and running streams mean to the soul of a man.' The luxuries I have taken for granted are now new discoveries for me. Opening the fridge to see green vegetables and fresh food just sitting there and waiting for me is an absolute joy. I open the fridge a lot during my first few days back home, often just for a look. Lights that come on with a switch; a toilet that flushes; water that comes from a tap; a hot shower – the luxuries of life that we all take for granted are truly appreciated, for a few days at least. Then everything returns to normal. How do you hold onto this sense of appreciation? And how can you feel as though you are doing at least some good in the world?

All things are changed by time. It is the journey that is crucial. That's what makes me embark on these adventures: the journey. The journey never ends. Your death will come soon enough – too quickly in fact – but the journey will be taken up and carried on by the like-minded. It is not about who or how many or how often or how quickly or how high. Life is to be enjoyed and lived, not bemoaned and complained about. We are so fortunate to be on this planet – to be alive. Each of us is nothing more than a fleck of dust in the passage of time. There is always time to get your life into perspective and live it. Attack life with the passion it demands.

For most, this will not require a trip to Antarctica. It may be something as simple as telling your mother that you love her, or telling your partner how much they mean to you. It may be walking further than you ever have before. It may be writing a letter to an old friend who you remember fondly but with whom you have lost contact. Make the effort and enjoy its rewards. Life – like this trek – is a wonderful journey. Don't miss it.

Last night at Patriot Hills

Horseshoe Valley from Patriot Hills

Chapter 13

WHERE ARE WE GOING?

As a group the Boss, Mertz and I managed to find our way back to Patriot Hills, out of Antarctica and ultimately back home. But now that I am back, I keep asking myself, 'Where are we going?' Humankind is the dominant species on the planet, capable of altering and determining the quality of the global environment and our lives. But how carefully are we exercising this power and are we looking to the future or merely satisfying our short-term interests? We find it easy to dismiss many of our fellow humans as arrogant, selfish, careless, aloof, egotistical, greedy, opportunistic, ignorant, disingenuous, abusive, devious, unscrupulous, immoral, ignorant, excessive or just plain wrong. These are not labels that we would like applied to ourselves, yet, as a species, they accurately describe so much of our behaviour in relation to our environment.

The next 'great war' is already being fought between those who seek to serve their own short-term interests and those seeking a sustainable future; the battleground will be climate change. Of course there have always been fluctuations in the climate of our planet, and there always will be, but the concern now is that many of these changes have been created by human activity. We have the ability, but do we have the will to alter our behaviour? Will today's great polluters and producers of carbon dioxide go the same way as asbestos miners and big tobacco companies? Will they continue to deny their impact on the health of the planet and its inhabitants in order to keep obscene profits flowing to their shareholders? When this state of denial proves unsustainable, will they then bicker over what restrictions should apply to whom? Will governments proudly announce that they will do all that they can to regulate the human effect on climate change so long as it does not disadvantage their respective economies? We must admit to our problem, address it, invest in solutions and put in the infrastructure now if we are to have any hope of victory in the centuries-long battle ahead. If we are to succeed in reducing our heavy footprint on the planet, then we have no time to squabble. But squabble we will.

A vehicle parked that is parked for too long in one place will attract a fine, but the same vehicle can spew tons of carbon dioxide into the atmosphere each year without ever attracting a fine. Which action is of greater detriment and concern to the community? Water costs less than one cent per litre and is in short supply. At the time of writing fuel for our motor vehicles is more than AUD$1.20 per litre. But which is ultimately more valuable? It makes you think: have we got our priorities in order? Why aren't polluters made to pay for their destruction? Will placing a real cost on emissions (thus making their businesses less profitable) send them scurrying in search of cleaner alternatives? How would such a policy be implemented and what would it look like?

Sir Nicholas Stern, head of the British Government Economic Service and former chief economist of the World Bank, recently issued his much-anticipated awaited report on climate change and what we can do about it. He has identified three components of an effective global response to stabilising, and ultimately reducing, the carbon dioxide in our atmosphere.

> The first is carbon pricing, through tax, trading or regulation, so that people pay the full social cost of their actions. The second is policy to support innovation and deployment of low-carbon technologies. The third is removal of barriers to energy efficiency and measures to inform, educate and persuade. Policies should tackle non-energy emissions as well, one third of the global total. Action to avoid further deforestation should be an urgent priority.

The problem can seem overwhelming, but it is not too late for action. Stern's research clearly shows that 'it is still possible to avoid the worst risks and impacts of climate change at an affordable cost, if well-designed and co-ordinated action at a national and global level is taken forward as a matter of urgency.'

So there is hope, but changes in attitude, a reassessment of how we produce energy and a change in practice are needed. While it can't hurt to think about the problem or to hope or pray or wish, we must also *do* something, and soon. Make meaningful changes in your lifestyle that will help to lessen your footprint on the planet. Make meaningful changes at your place of work. Be a leader, encouraging others to make changes to the way they behave.

You might be thinking that, as an individual, you cannot make a difference. You might be asking yourself, 'What use will my efforts be when China and India are producing so much pollution?' Nothing has ever been achieved in the history of humankind by thinking, 'If they won't do it, then we won't do it either.' Some ask why should we invest in new, clean energy technology when there is no guarantee of a return or success. Yet the same people happily invest hundreds of thousands of dollars in the education of their children with no guarantee of wisdom on completion. These people also invest millions in the stock market with no guarantee of a return, and think nothing of the high risks. These investments are not generally questioned because we deem them right and responsible for ourselves. A sustainable future is right and responsible for all.

Why can't Australia lead the world in renewable energy? Why can't Australia reward clean energy ideas and fund research? Are we so addicted to oil and coal that we can see nothing else? We have abundant sunshine capable of generating huge amounts of solar power, which could ease our reliance on fossil fuel. The roaring forties blast along our southern shores, providing ample opportunity to develop and improve wind-farming technology. Harnessing the power of the ocean, or more precisely wave energy, is largely untried but has huge potential. A report from CETO Wave Energy describes their new technology, which produces energy that is clean and renewable, with no emissions. Their invention is essentially a pump, which is attached to the ocean bed. A submerged buoy powers the device by harnessing the wave energy and transmitting it to the pump. The pump produces high pressure water, which is channelled ashore through a series of pipes to generate electricity through a turbine. It is then put through a reverse-osmosis desalination unit, producing fresh water. This is just one example of the available technologies – so simple yet so brilliant. Since 85 per cent of the Australian population live within 50 kilometres of the coast, it seems logical to harness the sea to provide clean energy and fresh water.

There must be many more under-resourced and undiscovered technologies just waiting to be embraced and developed. We must seek out, develop and adopt these sustainable technologies. Jeffery Immelt, Chairman and chief executive officer of General Electric says, 'We think green means green. This is a time period where environmental improvement is going to lead toward profitability.' As more leaders of business and government come to realise this fundamental truth – that informed public demand will drive change and ultimately profits in new and exciting business environments – they too will be swept up by the wave of public opinion that demands that we consume less, conserve more.

My journey through Antarctica reinforced my beliefs and caused me to reassess my priorities. Sir Nicholas Stern summed up his findings thus:

> Despite the size of the challenge, the findings of the review are essentially optimistic. If we act now, and work internationally, we can reduce the risks drastically at modest cost. But if we delay just 10 or 20 years, the costs will be much higher, and the risks much greater. With strong and urgent action, governments, businesses and individuals, working together, can safeguard our future growth and prosperity. We must not waste this opportunity. The future depends on what we decide now.

Travelling though rural and remote Australia, I have witnessed first hand the rise in salinity, our inefficient use of water, and the loss of habitat and biodiversity all since the arrival of white man a mere 220 years ago. Worldwide there are approximately 1.6 million described species to date with estimates of undescribed species ranging from 5 million to 50 million; the most optimistic estimates suggest that we have identified less than 20 per cent of the planet's biodiversity.

Imagine our country, our planet is the latest jet aircraft – the largest ever built, made up in part of many kilometres of wiring, hundreds of thousands of rivets and tons of paint.

The plane is brand new and sparkling until people arrive and begin to fly in it. It endures the knocks and bumps of a commercial life. A few rivets pop off. Are we still happy to fly? The paint chips and looks untidy – no worries! A few metres of wiring are suddenly missing. Another dozen rivets pop off. Pop! Pop! Pop! Another 50 disappear, then more.

At what point do you no longer wish to fly? When will a wing drop off? At what point do we say enough is enough? How far do we push on, because the 'plane must keep flying for the economic benefit of us all' while more and more rivets pop off? Can we afford to slow down and take the time to reinvest and repair some of the damage done? Some say that we cannot. A growing number of us, however, think that we should slow down and repair while we can or, alternatively, rebuild a smaller, renewable plane. It may not be as fast or as big but it may just serve us better and we may just have to get used to it.

We can continue to destroy or we can learn to change. The choice is ours.

Horseshoe Valley

ANTARCTICA: SOME FACTS

» **Winter population:** 1350

» **Summer population:** 5500

» **Tourist visitors:** 18 000–20 000 each summer. The vast majority of these visitors cruise the shoreline on ships.

» **Lowest recorded temperature:** –90°c at the Russian base Vostok on 21 July 1983 (during the dark winter).

» **Highest peak:** Mount Vinson, at 4900 metres.

» **Ice-free land:** 1 per cent.

» **Deepest drilled ice core:** 3.2 kilometres deep. This ice core is 950 000 years old at its base. The air bubbles found in such ice cores provide a record of the weather, pollution and natural events of our recent past.The continent is covered by ice that is 5 kilometres deep at its thickest points. The average depth of the ice coverage is approximately 3 kilometres. This astonishing amount of ice has been formed over millions of years by the build-up and compacting of snow.

» If all the ice contained in Antarctica were to melt, sea levels would rise by 60–70 metres.

» Antarctica holds 70 per cent of the Earth's fresh water as ice.

» Antarctica contains 90 per cent of the Earth's ice.

» Antarctica is slowly sinking under the weight of this ice. If the ice were to melt, the land mass would slowly rise again.

» NASA has tested their Martian vehicles in the dry valleys of Antarctica, as these valleys closely resemble the surface of Mars. The dry valleys have not received any rainfall for over two million years.

» The largest recorded iceberg – 300 kilometres long and almost 40 kilometres wide – was discovered in 2000 floating off the Ross Ice Shelf.

» During winter, the frozen sea ice doubles the size of Antarctica before melting again during the summer.

» Antarctica is considered a desert because of its lack of precipitation. It has a similar level of precipitation to the Sahara Desert – less than 5 centimetres a year.

» In 1998, NASA satellites recorded that the ozone hole over Antarctica, at 27 million square kilometres, was the largest ever recorded.

» Sledge dogs were banned from Antarctica in 1992 because of their impact on the environment.

» Antarctica is the windiest place on Earth, with recorded wind speeds reaching more than 300 kilometres per hour.

» There are no polar bears in Antarctica.

» Argentina, Australia, Chile, France, New Zealand, Norway and the United Kingdom all have territorial claims to large sections of Antarctica. These claims were made in the early part of the twentieth century and are not recognised by the USA or any of the other nations with bases on Antarctica.

» Copper, gold, nickel, platinum, iron ore, coal and other minerals have all been found in Antarctica but have not been discovered in commercial quantities.

» The Antarctic Treaty was signed in 1959 and came into effect in 1961. It establishes a legal framework for the continent's management, setting it aside as 'A natural reserve, devoted to peace and science'. Almost 50 member nations are signatories to the treaty. In broad terms, the treaty states that the area is to be used for peaceful means; it prohibits nuclear explosions, grants freedom of scientific investigation, and ensures protection of the environment, both sea and land.

» In 1991, 24 nations signed an agreement banning oil and mineral exploration in Antarctica until 2041.

» At 14 000 square kilometres, Lake Vostok is the largest of approximately 100 subterranean lakes in Antarctica. Lake Vostok lies beneath a 4-kilometre-thick ice sheet and has been locked up for over a million years. Scientists hope to discover isolated microbial life forms living here in the purest environment on the planet – life forms that have never been seen before. There are several theories about why the lake is not frozen: it is being kept warm by the geothermal heat from the Earth's interior; the thick ice sheet is acting as blanket of protection from the cold temperatures above; the lake did not freeze after a period of mild weather some 5000 years ago; it remains liquid because of the pressure from the ice above. The explanation could well be a combination of all of these or none at all. That's the thing: no one really knows. In 1999, Russian scientists halted their drilling for five years in order to review the drilling process. There were fears that the lake might become contaminated if drilling continued. Critics are still concerned that any leak or grime from the drill will destroy this pristine environment. The catch-22 is that the treasures of this unique environment cannot be revealed and studied without risk of destroying them. Drilling is scheduled to begin again in 2007.

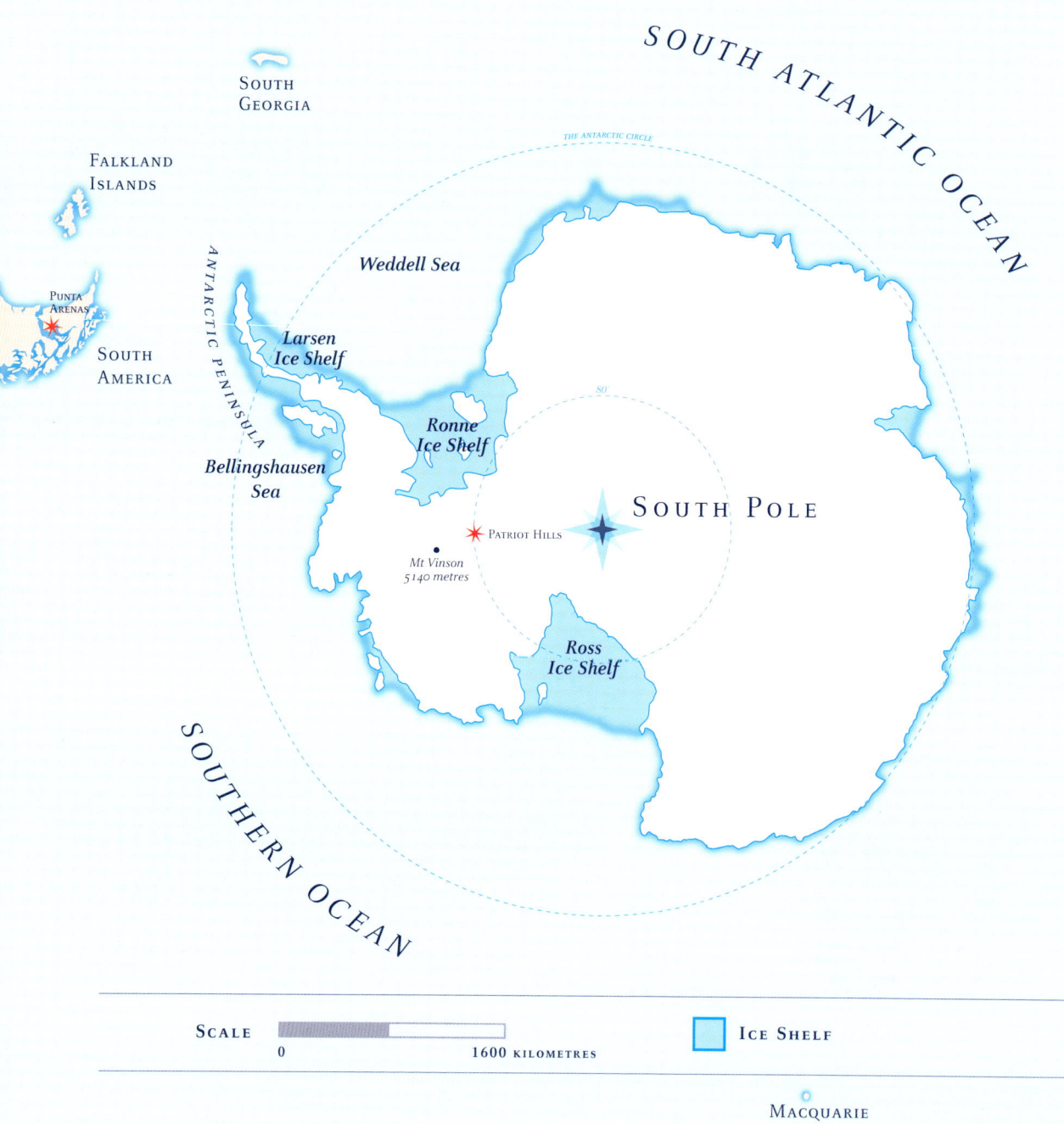

ANTARCTICA

SOUTH GEORGIA

FALKLAND ISLANDS

SOUTH ATLANTIC OCEAN

THE ANTARCTIC CIRCLE

Weddell Sea

PUNTA ARENAS

SOUTH AMERICA

ANTARCTIC PENINSULA

Larsen Ice Shelf

Ronne Ice Shelf

Bellingshausen Sea

80

PATRIOT HILLS

SOUTH POLE

Mt Vinson
5140 metres

Ross Ice Shelf

SOUTHERN OCEAN

SCALE

0   1600 KILOMETRES

ICE SHELF

MACQUARIE ISLAND

NEW ZEALAND

AUSTRALIA

AFRICA

NORTH AMERICA

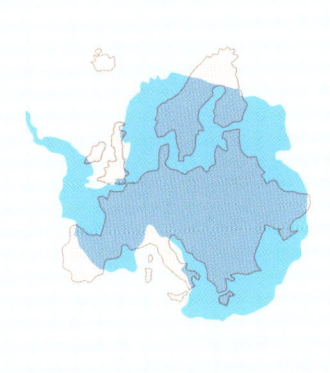

EUROPE

SOUTH AMERICA

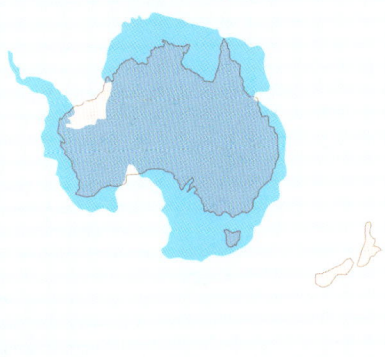

AUSTRALIA

CONVERSION CHART

METRIC TO IMPERIAL UNITS	IMPERIAL TO METRIC UNITS
1 centimetre = 0.394 inches	1 inch = 25.4 millimetres
1 metre = 3.28 feet	1 foot = 30.5 centimetres
1 kilometre = 0.621 mile	1 mile = 1.61 kilometres
$^\circ C = \frac{5}{9} \times (^\circ F - 32)$	$^\circ F = (\frac{9}{5} \times {}^\circ C) + 32$
1.85 kilometres per hour = 1 knot	1 knot = 1.85 kilometres per hour

NOTES ON SOURCES

The following books provided essential information on Antarctica and its history during the writing of this book:

Bickel, Lennard, *This Accursed Land*, Sun Books, Melbourne, 1978.

Cherry-Garrard, Apsley, *The Worst Journey in the World: Antarctic, 1910–1913*, Constable, London, 1922.

Headland, Robert, *Chronological List of Antarctic Expeditions and Related Historical Events*, Cambridge University Press, Cambridge, 1989.

Hillary, Peter & Elder, John E., *In the Ghost Country: A Lifetime Spent on the Edge*, Free Press, New York, 2003.

Huntford, Roland, *The Last Place on Earth: Scott and Amundsen's Race to the South Pole*, Hodder & Stoughton, London, 1979.

Hurley, Frank, *South with Endurance: Shackleton's Antarctic Expedition 1914–1917: The Photographs of Frank Hurley*, edited by Tamiko Rex, Simon & Schuster, New York, 2001.

Lansing, Alfred, *Endurance: Shackleton's Incredible Voyage to the Antarctic*, photography by Frank Hurley, Carroll & Graf, New York, 2000 [1959].

Martin, Stephen, *A History of Antarctica,* State Library of New South Wales Press, Sydney, 1996.

Mawson, Sir Douglas, *The Home of the Blizzard: A True Story of Antarctic Survival*, foreword by Ranulph Fiennes, St Martin's Press, New York, 1998 [1915].

Mickleburgh, Edwin, *Beyond the Frozen Sea: Visions of Antarctica*, Paladin Grafton, London, 1990.

Ousland, Børge, *Alone across Antarctica*, self-published, 1997.

Robert, Scott, *Scott's Last Expedition*, volume 1, *The Journals of Captain R. F. Scott*, Macmillan, London, 1913.

Rosove, Michael H., *Let Heroes Speak: Antarctic Explorers, 1772–1922*, Naval Institute Press, Annapolis, Maryland, 2000.

Shackleton, Sir Ernest, *The Heart of the Antarctic: Being the Story of the British Antarctic Expedition 1907–1909*, J. B. Lippincott Company, Philadelphia, 1909.

The following websites provided useful information on Antarctica and other topics covered in this book:

www.70south.com
An independent news and information website on Antarctica, with useful articles on a wide range of topics, including Antarctic history and wildlife.

www.antarctica.ac.uk
The website of the British Antarctic Survey.

www.antarctic-circle.org
A forum for scholars and knowledgeable amateurs interested in non-scientific Antarctic studies.

www.bbc.co.uk/history/historic_figures/
A useful database of information on a wide range of historic figures, including famous Antarctic explorers.

www.btinternet.com/˜sa_sa/south_georgia/south_georgia_history_20.html
A short history of South Georgia Island in the twentieth century.

www.capgo.com/Resources/InterestStories/WindChill/WindChill.html
A useful explanation of wind chill and how it is calculated.

www.chileaustral.com
Tourist information for visitors to Chile.

www.cia.gov/cia/publications/factbook/geos/ay.html
Information on Antarctica from the CIA's World Fact Book.

www.coolantarctica.com
   Pictures and general information on Antarctica.

www.ec.gc.ca/international/regorgs/antarctic/1antarctic_e.htm
   Useful information on Antarctica and the Antarctic Treaty System on the Meteorological
   Service of Canada website.

www.everesthistory.com
   Website dedicated to the history of mountaineering on Mount Everest.

www.framheim.com
   Website dedicated to all aspects of polar exploration.

www.gdargaud.net/Antarctica/index.html
   The website of Antarctic adventurers Guillaume and Jennifer Dargaud.

www.geoffsomers.co.uk
   Geoff Summers' website.

www.ousland.com
   Børge Ousland's website.

www.peterhillary.com
   Peter Hillary's website.

www.puntaarenas.com
   Information on Punta Arenas, including the town's history.

www.resa.net/nasa/antarctica.htm
   Information on Lake Vostok and the life forms that survive in the extreme Antarctic
   environment.

www.rgs.org/NR/rdonlyres/6F643E3F-3167-466F-ABED-95F6915FDE2C/0/PolarManual.pdf
   The Royal Geographic Society's polar expeditions manual.

www.royalnavalmuseum.org/research_info_sheets.htm
   Information sheets from the Royal Naval Museum in Portsmouth, including information
   on a number of Antarctic explorers.

www.sirpeterblaketrust.org
   Sir Peter Blake's website.

www.south-pole.com
   Website dedicated to the history of Antarctic exploration.

www.weatherimages.org
   Live weather images.

EXTENDED NOTES ON ILLUSTRATIONS

Pg 38 *En route with stores to Aladdin's Cave. Left to right: Mertz, Ninnis, Murphy.* Photographer: Frank Hurley, 1885–1962. Frame No: Home and Away 36623. Main Record: Australasian Antarctic Expedition, 1911–14: collection of Photographs. State Library of NSW.

Pg 39 *Sledging south from Cape Denison up the ice slopes. Mertz with the dog team.* Creator: Xavier Mertz, d.1913. Frame no: Home and Away –37046. Main Record: Australasian Antarctic Expedition, 1911–14: collection of Photographs. State Library of NSW.

Pg 40 *Mertz and Basilisk.* Creator: Laseron, Charles Francis. Frame No: Home and Away – 37188. Main Record: Australian Antarctic Expedition, 1911–14: collection of Photographs. State Library of NSW.

Pg 42 *Dr Mertz and a coastal ice formation near Cape Denison.* Creator: Hurley, Frank, 1885–1962. Frame No: Home and Away – 36714. Main Record: Australasian Antarctic Expedition, 1911–14: collection of Photographs. State Library of NSW.

Pg 42 *Mertz leaving the hut by the trapdoor on the verandah roof.* Creator: Hurley, Frank, 1885–1962. Frame No: Home and Away – 36468. Main record: Australasian Antarctic Expedition, 1911–14: collection of Photographs. State Library of NSW.

Pg 43 *The inscription on tablet below the memorial cross at Cape Denison.* Creator: Hurley, Frank, 1885–1962. Frame No: Home and Away – 36636. Main Record: Australasian Antarctic Expedition, 1911–14: collection of Photographs. State Library of NSW.

Pg 44 *Sir Ernest Henry Shackleton (1874–1922).* Photographer unidentified. Reference: F-8706-1/4. Alexander Turnbull Library, Wellington, NZ.

Pg 45 *Dr Edward Adrian Wilson (1872–1912), Robert Falcon Scott (1868–1912) and Sir Ernest Henry Shackleton (1874–1922), members of the British National Antarctic Expedition, starting for the Great South Journey. They left 02.11.1902 and returned on 02.02.1903.* Photographer unidentified. Collection Ref: PAColl-4225-01. Alexander Turnbull Library, Wellington, NZ.

Pg 46 *The Southern Sledging Party just returned.* Photographer: L.C. Bernacchi. Date: 05.02.1903. Image Number: S0014440. Royal Geographical Society.

Pg 47 *Members of the Shackleton Expedition and the Queen's Union Jack at the South Camp.* Photographer unidentified. Reference Number: F-8698-1/4. Alexander Turnbull Library, Wellington, NZ.

Pg 48 *Sir Ernest Shackleton (1874–1922) on board the 'Nimrod' after return from Antarctica on 04.03.1909.* Photographer unidentified. Reference Number: F-116771-1/2. Alexander Turnbull Library, Wellington, NZ.

Pg 50   *The 'Endurance' frozen into ice, Midwinter's Day 1910.* Photographer: James F Hurley (1890–1962). Reference Number: PAColl-2904-28. Alexander Turnbull Library, Wellington, NZ.

Pg 50   *The ship 'Endurance' crushed in ice, during the Trans-Antarctic Expedition (1914–1917).* Photographer: James F Hurley. Reference Number: F-8746-1/4. Alexander Turnbull Library, Wellington, NZ.

Pg 51   *Map of the 'Endurance' in Weddell Sea.* Date: 1914–1916. Image Number: S0010095. Royal Geographical Society.

Pg 52   *The temporary camp after the 'Endurance' was wrecked during Shackleton's expedition. Wilde and Ernest Henry Shackleton (1874–1922) in foreground.* Photographer: James F Hurley (1890–1962). Collection: T Orde Lees Collection. Alexander Turnbull Library, Wellington, NZ.

Pg 53   *Thomas Orde Haas Lees (1879–1952) and Charles J Green cooking in camp on the sea ice, Antarctica. Charles J Green was the cook on Shackleton's British Imperial Trans-Antarctic Expedition.* Photographer: James F Hurley (1890–1962). Reference Number: F-2934-1/4. Alexander Turnbull Library, Wellington, NZ.

Pg 53   *Ernest Henry Shackleton (1874–1922) and Harry (McNish) McNeish (1874–1930) alongside the stove at Patience Camp.* Photographer: James F Hurley. Collection: J Pontefract Album. Alexander Turnbull Library, Wellington, NZ.

Pg 54   *155. Camped under boat (Elephant Island)* British Imperial Trans-Antarctic Expedition, 1914–17. Order No: a423080. State Library of NSW.

Pg 55   *The hut made from upturned boats and tents by Shackleton's men, Elephant Island 1916. Shackleton and his men reached Elephant Island on 15.04.1916. The first officer, Lionel Greenstreet, and the official artist, George Marston, suggested that two of the boats,* Stancomb Wills *and* Dudley Docker *be converted into a hut. The boats were overturned and supported on stone walls with the remains of the tents acting as wind breaks. The men lived in this hut during the four months that it took Shackleton, using the remaining boat,* James Caird *to sail to South Georgia and return to rescue them.* Photographer: James F Hurley (1890–1962). Reference Number: PAColl-2904-60. Alexander Turnbull Library, Wellington, NZ.

Pg 55   *Launching the* James Caird *at Elephant Island for Shackleton's 800 mile voyage to South Georgia 24.04.1916.* Photographer: James F Hurley. Collection: T O H Lees Collection. Alexander Turnbull Library, Wellington, NZ.

Pg 56 *Kind Edward Cove South Georgia & Grytviken Whaling Station from where the Expedition started.* Photographer: Frank Hurley. Date: 1914–1917. Order Number: a285001. State Library of NSW.

Pg 57 *South Georgia Mountains.* Photographer: Frank Hurley. Date: 1914–1917. Image Number: S0011712. Royal Geographical Society.

Pg 58 *Ernest Shackleton and dignitaries at Punta Arenas.* Photographer: Frank Hurley. Date: 1914–1916. Image Number: S0015602. Royal Geographical Society.

Pg 59 *The rescuers and the rescued at Punta Arenas, in the Straits of Magellan, Chile. Captain Pardo in the centre (in uniform); Ernest Henry Shackleton (1874–1922) to left of Pardo (hand on shoulder); Wilde on Shackleton's left; Thomas Orde Hans Lees (1877–1958) on right of Pardo; George Edward Marston (1882–1940) separated by gap of two from Orde Lees 1916.* Photographer unidentified. Collection: T Orde Lees Collection. Alexander Turnbull Library, Wellington, NZ.

Pg 60 *Lawrence Edward Grace Oates (1880–1912). Captain 6th Inns. Dragoons. One of the party on Captain Robert Scott's expedition to the South Pole in 1910–1913. Perished in 1912.* Photographer: Herbert G Ponting (1870–1935). Collection: Joseph Kinsey Collection. Alexander Turnbull Library, Wellington, NZ.

Pg 62 *Studio Portrait of Captain Scott in dress uniform. The negative is from an original, which has been signed by him.* Photographer: John Thomson fl (1910–1921) London. Reference Number: F-8705-1/4. Alexander Turnbull Library, Wellington, NZ.

Pg 62 *Captain Roald Amundsen (1872–1928) Norwegian Antarctic Explorer, and with his team of men, made the first successful expedition to the South Pole in 1912.* Reference: F-8705-1/4. Alexander Turnbull Library, Wellington, NZ.

Pg 63 *Bunk beds belonging to Bowers, Cherry-Garrard, Oates, Meares and Aitkinson, during the British Antarctic (Terra Nova) Expedition of 1910–1913.* Photographer: Herbert G Ponting (1870–1935). Collection: Joseph Kinsey Collection. Alexander Turnbull Library, Wellington, NZ.

Pg 63 *Meares and Oates at the blubber stove.* Photographer: Herbert Ponting. Date: 26.05.1911 Image Number: S0004319. Royal Geographical Society.

Pg 64 *Captain Oates and ponies in stable.* Photographer: Herbert Ponting. Date: 26.05.1911. Image Number: S0004317. Royal Geographical Society.

Pg 65 *The* Terra Nova *and at big ice-foot.* Photographer: Herbert Ponting. Date: 16.01.1911. Image Number: S0004179. Royal Geographical Society.

Pg 65 *Captain Lawrence Edward Grace Oates (1880–1912) and some of the ponies, Antarctica.* Photographer: Herbert G Ponting (1870–1935). Collection: Scott Album.

Pg 66 *The pole party at the Norwegian tent, Antarctica.* Photographer: Henry R Bowers (1883–1912). Date: 1910–1912. Collection: Scott Album. Alexander Turnbull Library, Wellington, NZ.

Pg 67 *Members of the British Antarctic Expedition of 1910–1913 at the South Pole.* Photographer: Henry R Bowers. Date: 1910–1912. Reference Number: PA1-f-066-12-1. Alexander Turnbull Library, Wellington, NZ.

Pg 68 *Four men on skis pulling a laden sledge with another man pushing it. Taken during the 1907–1909 Shackleton Expedition.* Date: (Between 1907 and 1909). Photographer unidentified. Reference Number: F-8707-1/4. Alexander Turnbull Library, Wellington, NZ.

Pg 69 *Members of the British Antarctic Expedition of 1910–1913 leaving the 3 degrees depot.* Photographer: Henry Robertson Bowers (1883–1912). Date: 1910–1912. Collection reference: PA1-f-066-11-4. Alexander Turnbull Library, Wellington, NZ.

Pg 70 *The memorial cairn built by Debenham's party on the site of Robert Falcon Scott's tent in the Antarctic.* Photographer: Frank Debenham (1883–1965). Date: 1912. Collection: Scott Album. Alexander Turnbull Library, Wellington, NZ.

Pg 72 *Dr Atkinson's frostbitten hand.* Photographer: Herbert Ponting. Date: 05.07.1911. Image Number: S0004339. Royal Geographical Society.

Pg 72 *Sledging ration. One man's ration for 1 day.* Photographer: Herbert G Ponting (1870–1935). Date: 1910–1912. Collection: Scott Album. Alexander Turnbull Library, Wellington, NZ.

ACKNOWLEDGEMENTS

Peter Hillary and Jason Veale who made the dream of Antarctic travel possible and without whom I would have no story to tell. Thank you for all your laughter and patience.

Special thanks to John Elder and Peter Hillary for allowing me to quote from their book *In The Ghost Country*. For more information go to www.peterhillary.com

To our adopted namesakes: Shackleton, Oates and Mertz. Thank you for your inspiration.

My office manager and research assistant Lynn Freebairn – well done and thank you.

The team at Traffic Design – Deb, Sarah and Kelsey – thank you for bringing it all together.

Thank you to Josh Yeldham, Wendy Touhy, Peter Lothian, Tony Doubidoun and Jonar Nader for all the advice, corrections and direction along the way.

The team at Hardie Grant Books – Sandy Grant, Rod Morrison, Jasmin Chua, Keiran Rogers and Julie Pinkham. Thank you for getting me over the line.

Lucy Davison, thank you for making my words better.

To my parents Connie and Craig and my sister Chloe, thank you for your neverending love and support.

Thank you to my wife Caroline and daughter Florence for believing in me.

A particular thank you to Caroline for her patience, advice, understanding, input and proofreading. Without your generous love and support this would book would not have happened. You are the greatest!

This Acursed Land

In The Ghost Country

BIOGRAPHY

Jason Kimberley is a self-taught photographer with a passion for travel, adventure and capturing all that is wonderful and unique about landscapes and life. His first, self-published book, *Australia Exposed* (2003), was the result of a year-long 4WD trip around Australia in 2000 with his wife Caroline. The photographs were taken with his beloved 25-year-old SLR 35mm camera that has been on loan from his mother since 1982.

Prior to this Jason had a successful career in the retail industry working in sales, product design and manufacturing. He has worked in management for Country Road and the Just Jeans Group. He also ventured into the competitive Melbourne restaurant scene with the Veludo, in St Kilda, which quickly became one of the city's top-rated eateries.

Jason's love of travel was formed at an early age, after his family embarked on their first outback adventure in 1977. Since then he has travelled extensively throughout Australia and subjected himself to a number of demanding challenges including climbing South America's highest peak, Mount Aconcagua (22 840 ft), trekking Denali, and a month-long kayaking odyssey on Prince William Sound, both in Alaska. He has also canoed through the Peruvian Amazon. In 2006 Jason was commissioned to photograph aboard the yacht *Epsilon*'s Darwin to Broome leg of its circumnavigation of Australia, recreating the 1802–1804 voyage of Matthew Flinders to assist in raising funds for Alzheimer's research. In 2007 Jason was invited to join, then inducted as a member, of the prestigious Explorers Club – New York.

The summer of 2005/06 saw Jason spend 16 days in Antarctica at 80 degrees south with his travelling companions Jason Veale and Peter Hillary.

In January 2007 Jason's photographic exhibition was the opening event on the Australia Week calendar at the G'Day LA Celebrations in Los Angeles.

Jason lives in Melbourne with his wife Caroline and their daughter Florence.

www.sunburntcountry.net